AUTHENTICATION PROCESS

Connecting the Dots of Being a Believer and Living a Life of Purpose

Brinda Devine

EVANGELINE PUBLISHING

EVANGELINE PUBLISHING

Copyright © 2020 by Brinda Devine

FIRST EDITION

For permission requests, contact the author at: bddevine@gmail.com or 248-219-6685

www.brindadevine.com

EVANGELINE PUBLISHING | FARMINGTON HILLS, MICHIGAN

ISBN: 978-0-9974044-1-8
Library of Congress Control Number: 2019914381

Printed and bound in the United States of America

Text design by www.tothepointsolutions.com

*I dedicate this second book to God, the Holy Spirit,
and Jesus Christ, my Lord and Savior.
Thank you for opening my mind and my heart.*

*I also dedicate this book to a good friend, Sue Simmers,
who lived a life of purpose. Full of energy and a passion for
helping people, her good works touched everyone she met,
both in Royal Oak, Michigan, and Cameroon, Africa.
Sue, we love you and miss you.*

Contents

SECTION III: FOLLOW HIM

Acknowledgments

Thank you to my husband, Eddie, and son, Elijah, for giving me the space and time to do what I want to do. I love you.

Thank you to my spiritual sister Heidi, for reading my initial draft and seeing more.

Thank you to my spiritual sisters of Purpose 8.

**Connecting the dots of being a Believer
and living a life of purpose**

Peter is Introduced to His Weakness

Luke 22:54-62, ESV

Then they seized him and led him away, bringing him into the high priest's house, and Peter was following at a distance. And when they had kindled a fire in the middle of the courtyard and sat down together, Peter sat down among them. Then a servant girl, seeing him as he sat in the light and looking closely at him, said, "This man also was with him." But he denied it saying, "Woman, I do not know him." And a little later someone else saw him and said, "You also are one of them." But Peter said, "Man, I am not." And after an interval of about an hour, still another insisted saying, "Certainly this man also was with him, for he too is a Galilean." But Peter said, "Man, I do not know what you are talking about." And immediately, while he was still speaking, the rooster crowed. And the Lord turned and looked at Peter. *And Peter remembered the saying of the Lord*, how he had said to him, "Before the rooster crows today, you will deny me three times." And he went out and wept bitterly.

God is Renewing Us for His Purpose

Philippians 2:12-13, ESV

Therefore, my beloved, as you have always obeyed, so now, not only as in my presence but much more in my absence, *work out your own salvation with fear and trembling*, for it is God who works in you, both to will and to work for His good pleasure.

Introduction

In the spring of 2015, I graduated from Ambassador Bible Training School (ABTS), a two-year Bible study class sponsored by my church, Family Victory Fellowship Church, and Pastors Larry and Sylvia Jordan. I was on a journey to discover my purpose, which was to find out why God created me and the plans He had for my life. My experience at ABTS was life-changing and it showed me that being a Believer was more than just going to church and hoping that I would get into Heaven. My life was to be about loving and serving the Lord, and helping people—and not just Believers, but people.

Now, I don't know about everybody else, but once I gave my life to God, I became full and had a desire to please Him. Yet, there was a problem. I was full and open to learning more and doing more, but there was no soft pad to land on. I wanted to take this new fullness and use it somewhere, but I didn't know what to do with it. I mean, I was saved, but what do I do next? How do I take the Christian principle of purpose and apply it to my life? How do I connect the dots?

I asked a few people I trusted and who I thought would have the answer. They did not. During this time, I was also praying to God and asking the Holy Spirit to tell me what my purpose was. I prayed intermittently and waited for some great sign that would tell me what I was supposed to do. As I noted in my first book, *Discover Your Value, Discover Your Purpose*, "One Sunday, when I was in the car with my family, we were just about to turn into the church parking lot, when the Holy Spirit revealed to me my purpose. There was no loud crack of thunder or bolt of lightning—but I was listening and I heard. The Holy Spirit revealed that He wanted me to tell others the importance of discovering their value and God's purpose for them—and that is what I have been doing for the past three years. There may be other things God wants of me, I don't know. But at this moment, I am doing what He has given me.

Now, I am going to be honest. I struggled with what the Holy Spirit asked me to do. But in the end, God always wins. Because I have a Type A personality, I wanted to just jump in and do something, but the Holy Spirit reminded me that I was a novice and not yet prepared to do what God wanted me to do. I needed to learn more so as not to cause harm or misdirect anyone. The Bible verses below support time for our preparation:

> 1 Timothy 3:6 ESV: He must not be a recent convert, or he may become puffed up with conceit and fall into the condemnation of the devil.

> 2 Timothy 3:16–17 ESV: All Scripture is breathed out by God and profitable for teaching, for reproof, for correction, and for training in righteousness, that the man of God may be complete, equipped for every good work.

> 2 Timothy 2:15 ESV: Be diligent to present yourself approved to God as a workman who does not need to be ashamed, accurately handling the word of truth.

Even though I was full, committed, and eager to do what God called me to do, I was still a novice trying to connect the dots. I wanted to keep learning, and even considered attending more Christian-based classes. Instead, I ended up taking notes on my spiritual and emotional renewing process (didn't know that is what was going on at the time) and those notes, along with direction from the Holy Spirit, led to me write *Discover Your Value, Discover Your Purpose*. By then I had gotten into the habit of writing in the morning and I needed something to keep me accountable to my purpose, so I started a blog on Facebook called *Daily Application/Discover Your Purpose8* where I shared my journey and posted on different topics focused on the importance of discovering our individual purpose. I didn't know it then, but the Bible study and Facebook posts were preparing me for what was ahead.

God's will is found by submitting your life to His purpose and using your spiritual gifts, natural talents, and skills to accomplish your assignment(s). While living a life of purpose, you will be continually tested with life's challenges and struggles and you will be given the opportunity to decide whether you will be righteous or not.

Some people call these life challenges and struggles *tests, trials, renewal, purging, personal breakthroughs,* or *taking off the old man and putting on the new*. In this book, I call these lifelong challenges and struggles the **authentication process**, because they authenticate who I say I am and my commitment to living a life of purpose.

Some of our challenges and struggles can be attributed to spiritual warfare. But some are also driven by our personal weaknesses, as Jesus' disciple Peter experienced as told in Luke 22:54–62. We read that Peter denies Jesus three times, just like Jesus said he would. Peter was so caught up in his immediate challenge/struggle that he didn't realize that he was denying Jesus. Look closer in this challenge/struggle. Peter is introduced to his weakness and he is ashamed that he has denied his Lord and Savior, not just once, but three times. Peter learned what Jesus already knew; that he was weak. And that is what happens to each of us, we show up to our tests as ourselves (full of our intellect, attitudes, perspectives, beliefs, distractions, fears, and personal hurts) instead of as a righteous, authentic Believer living a life of purpose.

It took a while for me to understand my own authentication process. Here's how it unraveled: One day, after going through a challenge at work, I re-read thoughts I had written in a digital journal on my iPhone. I looked over the dates and realized that over a two-year period, I had experienced, for the most part, the same type of challenge at least three times, although rewrapped to look new. During each challenge, I did not notice my weakness, only the injustice I believed I was experiencing. I was so out of order that in anger, I asked God in prayer to cast down my enemies and make them my footstools. I was totally wrong in my approach and, eventually, discovered through the Holy Spirit that the issue was not the challenge, but my response to the challenge. I was allowing my pride to distort who I confessed to be, a Believer, living a life of purpose.

The authentication process is a lifetime journey. No one on this earth is perfect; no one expects you to score 100% on each and every challenge or struggle you encounter in life. I believe the goal for us, as Believers, is to recognize and acknowledge our weaknesses and allow ourselves to lean on and depend on God to handle every situation.

When I learned to lean on and depend on God's strength instead of my own, the weight of my challenge/struggles lightened, life felt easier, and my energy and perspective shifted from the challenge/struggle to become the authentic person God called me to be.

I pray that as you encounter your own authentication process, you press to learn more about God and yourself, that you encourage yourself. There will be days when you wonder what is going on, why has your life become more difficult, why have old wounds and hurts arisen? And there will also be days when you are encircled in God's love and peace you never thought could be possible.

I encourage you to keep a journal of your personal journey. As you go through your authentication process, these notes will provide you with evidence of your own weaknesses and hopefully the encouragement in knowing that God is pulling you through every one of life's challenges and struggles.

So, how do you connect the dots? How do you live an authentic life of purpose? Here are some suggestions:

1. Keep living.

2. Acknowledge that your own authentication process will be a lifelong process where you will experience good and bad times and your own set of personal weaknesses, just like the Disciple Peter.

3. Keep a personal journal where you write/type out your experiences and thoughts as they occur. Don't edit what you have written, leave your words as they are so that you retain your original thoughts and experience.

4. Be aware of destructive patterns and the parts you play in them, and learn the lesson within the patterns. Hindsight is 20/20. Look back over each challenge/struggle. You were being tested over and over with the same weaknesses, but under different circumstances. Identify the weakness and learn the lesson through prayer, revelation, study, and application of God's Word over your life.

5. As you learn the lessons and apply them to each new challenge/struggle, you will begin to see the layers of the old you pull away and the new, righteous, authentic you God created start to emerge.

The journey of authentication you are on, or about to embark on, is not easy. For me, it has been emotionally difficult. But, with each challenge/struggle, I have gotten better at recognizing my weaknesses and submitting my concerns to God. I am sharing my journey of authentication with you because I believe there is a huge disconnect in our church culture in teaching Believers: 1) how to apply God's Word in their everyday lives and 2) the message of purpose. For example, in church we often hear sermons about loving God, loving our neighbor, and serving God—but how could I apply and extend God's Word to my neighbor when I didn't even love *myself*? I needed help connecting the dots—but how do I connect sitting on a church pew to living a life of purpose?

No one told me what this journey would be like, and I am not suggesting that your authentication process will be the same as mine. I am simply telling you what occurred to me and the lessons I learned along the way that helped me connect the dots of being a Believer and living a life of purpose.

I am hopeful that this book will help you connect your own dots as you journey through your own authentication process, which is ultimately allowing God to remove the old and bring forth the new, righteous, authentic you created for purpose.

This book is organized in three sections with multiple chapters. Each section is a collection of my thoughts gathered from my journal; the chapters cover various topics I experienced on my journey in pursuit of purpose. My challenges, struggles and weaknesses have actually been the catalyst that helped me connect the Christian principle of purpose to my authentication process. Within each chapter are supportive Christian Bible Scriptures, a suggested application, and an area where you can write down your thoughts on what you have read in relation to your own journey.

SECTION I: BIRTH OF A RENEWED MIND

In this section, I grow spiritually. I have a desire to read, study, and apply God's Word to my life. There is a mindset shift from doing what Brinda wants to do, to listening to the Holy Spirit and being obedient.

I believe this is one of the Believer's biggest struggles, as Ephesians 4:22-24 says, "to put off your old self which belongs to your former manner of life and is corrupt through deceitful desires, and to be renewed in the spirit of your minds, and to put on the new self—created after the likeness of God in true righteousness and holiness."

*To have a mind like Christ, I mean, really, how do you change thoughts you have held for decades? How do you stop thinking as a singular being and start thinking about your life simply as an instrument to do God's will and praise Him? Let me be clear, it is not easy by any stretch of the imagination to change your mindset, but it can be done by first consistently submitting your life and will to God and applying His Word to your life every day, one day at a time. Chapter One shares my thoughts on my biggest obstacle in life: getting over **me**.*

Chapter One

Me

~ ⚬ ~

Connecting the dots: It's not about what I want. It's about what God wants.

Note 1: The biggest obstacle we face in life is ourselves. We judge and compare ourselves to others. We listen and agree with fear. We second-guess ourselves; we think we are not good enough. We tell ourselves not now, but later. We put everyone and everything first, instead of God. We are stubborn and prideful over small things. We walk into life and easily accept expectations created by our parents, our jobs, social media, and the world at large. We don't want to forgive. We think everything is about us. We listen, but don't really hear because we are insecure. We speak over others to defend ourselves, oftentimes when some words should be left unsaid. We waste time. We struggle to say simple words like "hello," "I'm sorry," "thank you," and "I appreciate you." We live a small life because we think small. We choose to follow someone we don't know to nowhere instead of following Jesus Christ who is our Lord and Savior.

Note 2: Honesty is an important element in discovering our value and purpose. To establish, or strengthen, our relationship with God, we must pray, study, be faithful, seek God's will, and be obedient to the revelations of the Holy Spirit. But within that process—hopefully, at the beginning—we have to be honest with ourselves. We have to dig through our pride, insecurities, hurt, attitude, me-isms, and whatever else is blocking us and have real and honest conversations with ourselves and with God. We need to allow Him to take control of our lives and direct us to our purpose. God's love encourages us to see ourselves as valuable, which in turn encourages us to want to please Him and discover our purpose. But first, we must be honest with ourselves.

Note 3: When you live a lifestyle (i.e., what you say, do, and think) that does not acknowledge God or agrees with His Word, then you have already made the choice that you will serve the devil. You don't have to confess with your mouth that you serve the devil, how you see yourself and treat people says it for you.

Note 4: Less of me Lord and more of you. In my thoughts. In my words. How I respond. Help me see others as You see them. Let me be the person you want and not what I want. Reset me today, Lord, and make me more like you.

Following are several Bible Scriptures to help support your new "me."

BIBLE SCRIPTURES

Ephesians 4:22–24 ESV, to put off your old self which belongs to your former manner of life and is corrupt through deceitful desires, and to be renewed in the spirit of your minds, and to put on the new self, created after the likeness of God in true righteousness and holiness.

Romans 8:5 ESV, For those who live according to the flesh set their minds on the things of the flesh, but those who live according to the Spirit set their minds on the things of the Spirit.

Philippians 2:3–4 ESV, Do nothing from selfish ambition or conceit, but in humility count others more significant than yourselves. Let each of you look not only to his own interests but also to the interests of others.

Galatians 6:3 ESV, For if anyone thinks he is something, when he is nothing, he deceives himself.

APPLICATION

We all have days when we are not our best and have missed the mark. But, guess what? You have the ability to hit your reset button and refocus on God's will and not your own. This is how I re-focus:

1. Acknowledge that I need some Word for my situation.

2. Open and honest prayer in that I acknowledge my weakness (usually pride) and ask for forgiveness.

3. Change my expectations from "God, do this for me" to "Yes, Lord, I will do what you want me to do."

4. Apply God's Word and the Holy Spirit's revelation over my situation.

5. Activate my faith. Trust that God is faithful and get past my apprehension or fear and believe what God says about me. Know that each day we are given the gift of life is another opportunity to do better. Reset, re-focus, and keep believing and living your life of purpose.

Related topic: Chapter Thirteen, Be Better

CHAPTER NOTES

Here is your chance to write down a few thoughts of your own before we go to the next chapter.

_____

_____

_____

_____

_____

_____

_____

_____

_____

_____

_____

_____

_____

_____

_____

_____

_____

_____

_____

Chapter Two

Distractions

⌘∽ ∼⌘

Connecting the dots: Open your eyes and be conscious of what and who is distracting you.

Note 1: I was thinking about distractions and how we allow them to define, bind, and limit us. My definition of a distraction is anything—a person, a personal hurt, a sickness, an attitude, a behavior, or an emotion/perception—that you allow to interfere with your relationship with God. We have so many responsibilities and priorities in our lives, but none should be greater than our relationships with God. I know you are busy, me too.

We all have so much going on in our lives—family, work, obligations, stress, etc. Some days, it's like we can't see the forest for the trees. Imagine yourself in a wide, open plain. Looking toward the horizon, you see a forest of tall, wide trees that represent your distractions. You want to get to the other side of the forest to establish or strengthen your relationship with God, but you can't because your distractions are so tall, wide, and pressed together they block your vision.

If you want to get closer to God, spend some time with yourself and discover the distractions that are keeping you from what God has just for you—love, value, and purpose. Life is so much easier when you allow God to direct your life instead of your distractions.

Note 2: If you would just allow yourself to stop denying how personal hurts, disappointments, and fears have bound you. Allow yourself to peel back all the layers that you call you. If you would just peel back the layers until you reach that place of child-like innocence; that level of consciousness where it is just you and God; that place where you realize you are just a spirit, a puff of vapor; here today, gone tomorrow; and He is the sovereign God, the Creator of all, including you. If you could just, this once, allow yourself to enter into His presence without any weight of the world, and for a bit of time, see the person He wants you to be rather than the flesh you run after.

If you pulled back that layer, you would begin to see how great you are, and each day you would see a little more of what God sees in you, what He had in mind before the world began. If you would just allow yourself to peel back those layers and trust God, you would soon be amazed at what was found: a person being filled with love, power, authority, and blessed with talents and spiritual gifts, all given to do His will. Your past will become less important, your heart will open, and your mind will focus on what is really important in this life: answering God's call and discovering and doing the purpose you were so wondrously created to do.

Note 3: Many of us long for acceptance, love, and care. God, our Father, can heal every heart, mend every hurt, wipe away every tear, hold us in every situation, and provide for all of our needs and wants. Recognize sad and hurtful childhood experiences for what they truly are, distractions. Stop falling for the same trick: the devil using your emotions and your past to distract you from what is ahead of you. If he can get you to keep looking back, you will never make any progress. Find your comfort in the Lord. Lay down your past. Bind it up in the power and authority of Jesus Christ our Lord and Savior and leave it in the past. And when you are free, don't just stand still. Walk forward and step into that spacious place that God holds just for you.

Note 4: Recognize that the devil (using your weaknesses—pride, insecurity, selfishness, anger, fear, etc.) comes to steal your joy, your peace, your love, your faith, and your purpose.

Note 5: Distractions. We make this so difficult to understand when, really, it's not. God created us because He loves us. He designed and made each of us for a purpose that is to be fulfilled. We have the freewill to ignore that purpose or to fulfill it. You may not like or want your purpose, but it is still yours to fulfill. You cannot fulfill your purpose until you decide to surrender your will and life to Him. The surrender is a daily, moment-to-moment process to abandon things, people, situations, emotions, bad habits, personal baggage, and the like that distract you from God and your purpose. We allow distractions because it is easier for us to deal with what we are comfortable with rather than agree with God and accept His infinite love.

Following are several Bible Scriptures to help you face and conquer the distractions that are keeping you bound and lacking in your relationship with God.

BIBLE SCRIPTURES

Galatians 5:16–26 ESV, But I say, walk by the Spirit, and you will not gratify the desires of the flesh. For the desires of the flesh are against the Spirit, and the desires of the Spirit are against the flesh, for these are opposed to each other, to keep you from doing the things you want to do. But if you are led by the Spirit, you are not under the law. Now the works of the flesh are evident: sexual immorality, impurity, sensuality, idolatry, sorcery, enmity, strife, jealousy, fits of anger, rivalries, dissensions, divisions, envy, drunkenness, orgies, and things like these. I warn you, as I warned you before, that those who do such things will not inherit the kingdom of God. But the fruit of the Spirit is love, joy, peace, patience, kindness, goodness, faithfulness, gentleness, self-control; against such things there is no law. And those who belong to Christ Jesus have crucified the flesh with its passions and desires. If we live by the Spirit, let us also keep in step with the Spirit. Let us not become conceited, provoking one another, envying one another.

James 4:1–17 ESV, What causes quarrels and what causes fights among you? Is it not this that your passions are at war within you? You desire and do not have, so you murder. You covet and cannot obtain, so you fight and quarrel. You do not have, because you do not ask. You ask and do not receive, because you ask wrongly, to spend it on your passions. You adulterous people! Do you not know that friendship with the world is enmity with God? Therefore whoever wishes to be a friend of the world makes himself an enemy of God.

Mark 7:21–23 ESV, For from within, out of the heart of man come evil thoughts, sexual immorality, theft, murder, adultery, coveting, wickedness, deceit, sensuality, envy, slander, pride, foolishness. All these evil things come from within, and they defile a person.

APPLICATION

We all have distractions, personal issues, hurt, and disappointments in our lives; some are more recognizable than others. People can encourage you for a lifetime, but until you decide to step out of fear and be courageous to address each and every one of your distractions, it is not going to make a difference. You will continue to be bound to the past. Be courageous and move forward.

Related topics: Chapter Nine, Fear and Chapter Fourteen, Struggles

CHAPTER NOTES

Here is your chance to write down a few thoughts of your own before we go to the next chapter.

_____

_____

_____

_____

_____

_____

_____

_____

_____

_____

_____

_____

_____

_____

_____

_____

_____

_____

_____

Chapter Three

I Am Valuable

⚬⟊⟊~ ~⟊⟊⚬

Connecting the dots: You are exactly what God says you are—"fearfully and wonderfully made."

Note 1: Many of us don't ask ourselves, What am I worth? What is my value? And yet, each day we communicate how we feel about ourselves and we don't even know it. We communicate how we perceive our value in the way we speak, behave, and think; and, ultimately, in how we live and treat other people.

Note 2: Your value has nothing to do with: How you look. The house you live in or the car you drive. Your marital status or if you have a mate. How long or short your hair is—or if you even have hair. How much money you have or don't have. Your job title. Whether you are young or old, a millennial or old-school. Your race or the color of your skin. Your talents or learned skills. Your education or lack of it. How well you speak or if you can mesmerize a crowd. Whether your clothes are new or purchased at the Salvation Army. Who likes you and who doesn't. How you feel about yourself and your place in life has everything to do with how you love and treat yourself and others.

Note 3: It's funny how we easily allow other people to define and label us, but we are apprehensive and even afraid to find out how God values and claims us through His Word.

Note 4: You should never have to convince anyone of your value. Your value was established by God before you were even born. No other opinion, including yours, really matters. Stop listening to negative people. Stop accepting no as the final answer. Stop accepting titles and names that don't belong to you. Stop caring about what people think about you. Stop standing still. Stop reliving the past. Stop procrastinating. Stop settling for less. Stop doubting yourself and the power and authority you hold. Stop trying to conform to this world and hold onto your value.

Note 5: Too few of us realize we are valuable and instead we choose to believe the lies the devil whispers to us, instead of the truth God proclaims. You always have a choice. Get rid of the negative story the devil keeps telling you about your future and replace it with the story God has already written for you. In the Bible, God tells us, you are loved and fearfully and wonderfully made. You can do all things. You are a conqueror. You are the head and not the tail. No weapon formed against you shall prosper. And, that all things work together for good for those that love the Lord and are called according to His purpose.

Note 6: When you know and are active in your purpose, you find direction and clarity in living. Your days will be focused on your purpose in some form. Each day we are bombarded with news and advertising (media, social media, friends, family, etc.) telling us who we should be; what we should buy; and, the most dangerous—how we should think and feel. Knowing how much God loves you gives you value. Once you know your value and purpose, you will tend to stay on topic and direct your actions, feelings, and thoughts toward your purpose.

Note 7: I am valuable simply because my God says I am. He is faithful and His Word never returns void with empty promises (Isiah 55:11).

Following are several Bible Scriptures to help you realize how much God loves you and how that love should shape how you feel about and see yourself.

BIBLE SCRIPTURES

Psalm 139:13–16 ESV, For you formed my inward parts; you knitted me together in my mother's womb. I praise you, for I am fearfully and wonderfully made. Wonderful are your works; my soul knows it very well. My frame was not hidden from you, when I was being made in secret, intricately woven in the depths of the earth. Your eyes saw my unformed substance; in your book were written, every one of them, the days that were formed for me, when as yet there was none of them.

John 3:16 ESV, For God so loved the world, that He gave His only Son, that whoever believes in Him should not perish but have eternal life.

1 Corinthians 6:19–20 ESV, Or do you not know that your body is a temple of the Holy Spirit within you, whom you have from God? You are not your own, for you were bought with a price. So glorify God in your body.

Isaiah 55:11 ESV, so shall my word be that goes out from my mouth; it shall not return to me empty, but it shall accomplish that which I purpose, and shall succeed in the thing for which I sent it.

Ecclesiastics 2:11 ESV, Then I considered all that my hands had done and the toil I had expended in doing it, and behold, all was vanity and a striving after wind, and there was nothing to be gained under the sun.

APPLICATION

I am convinced that if we all knew how valuable we are, and our purpose, the happier we would be. I found both value and purpose, and my life has changed so much for the better. Am I perfect? No, but I am so much better. When I say I found value, this is what I mean:

- I found out that God loves me. Proof: He gave His Son's life for me (John 3:16)

- I found out that He had me in mind before the foundation of the earth, He knows me inside and out. Proof: He made me (Psalm 139:13–16)

Because God loves me so much, that love gives me a measure of my value that far exceeds anything a person's words or actions can ever dictate about me. What does value look like? Value looks like you. God's love is the foundation, it is the standard, and it defines your value. It is simply this: God loves you, so you are valuable. So, do not accept the world's definition of love, acceptance, or value. The world (family, friends, social media, politics, fashion, technology, culture, old school, new school, etc.) and its desires are fleeting. But God's Word stands forever.

Related topics: Chapter Four, I Know Who I Am and Chapter Eight, Conform

CHAPTER NOTES

Here is your chance to write down a few thoughts of your own before we go to the next chapter.

_____

_____

_____

_____

_____

_____

_____

_____

_____

_____

_____

_____

_____

_____

_____

_____

_____

_____

Chapter Four

I Know Who I Am

⁕⁓ ⁓⁕

Connecting the dots: I am not who or what people say I am. No, I am much more. I am a Child of God.

Note 1: You will always come in contact with people who do not like you. You will always come across people who try to fit you into their miserable box. You will always meet people who are as fake as a $3 bill, and they want you to be just like them. You will always have to deal with somebody who thinks they are Fortune 500 material and you are simply bargain basement. Because of this, it is important for you to know whose you are and who you are because knowing this confirms your value and how you see yourself. God loves you. You are His Child and He has plans for your life—so truly, you are valuable and have a purpose.

Here is the danger if you don't know whose you are or who you are: when you refuse to accept and proclaim the value that God has prescribed for you, you leave yourself open to allowing other people to define you; write your story; label you; and eventually, restrict you. Once you accept the world's label—the world and all its false measures of success—you can be led anywhere. "My sheep hear my voice, and I know them, and they follow me" (John 10:27).

Note 2: "Beware of false prophets, who come to you in sheep's clothing, but inwardly are ravenous wolves. You will recognize them by their fruits. Are grapes gathered from thorn bushes or figs from thistles? So, every healthy tree bears good fruit, but the diseased tree bears bad fruit. A healthy tree cannot bear bad fruit, nor can a diseased tree bear good fruit. Every tree that does not bear good fruit is cut down and thrown into the fire. Thus, you will recognize them by their fruits" (Matthew 7:15-20).

Be careful of the company you keep; especially the people (family, friends, bosses, coworkers, neighbors, etc.) who try to devalue you and define you. In today's culture, people try to be politically correct and choose words that do not appear to offend the listener, but the intent is still there between the lines. If you are not careful, you may start to believe the subtle lies they tell and little by little, you will begin to doubt yourself, your value, and your purpose.

You and I are Children of God. We can do anything that God wills and that He gives us strength to do. Keep encouraging yourself, keep reading and studying your Bible, keep stepping forward with God. Ignore negative people, their noise and their lies. They do not know us and they certainly do not know our God, His sovereign power, nor the plans He has for our lives.

Note 3: One of the worst things I can ever do is to allow someone to define me; and then in my head and heart, agree to their worldly assessment. The only measure that matters to me is that God sees me as His child.

Following are several Bible Scriptures to help solidify your identity in God's kingdom and ultimately how much you mean to Him.

BIBLE SCRIPTURES

1 Corinthians 3:16–17 ESV, Do you not know that you are God's temple and that God's Spirit dwells in you? If anyone destroys God's temple, God will destroy him. For God's temple is holy, and you are that temple.

Galatians 4:7 ESV, So you are no longer a slave, but a son, and if a son, then an heir through God.

1 Peter 2:9 ESV, But you are a chosen race, a royal priesthood, a holy nation, a people for His own possession, that you may proclaim the excellences of Him who called you out of darkness into His marvelous light.

APPLICATION

When you were a child, people labeled you. As an adult, people put you in a category. In school and at work, someone probably told you 'No, you stay here. You can't do or be that.' After years of hearing and experiencing what someone else thinks, some of us just slide into a groove and stay in our spots, our boxes, our place; afraid to push the boundaries and discover who we really are: a Child of God who was created to bring others to Christ and live a life of purpose.

For many people, that last sentence can be scary because it means they will have to do something, they will have to be fearless and they will have to be faithful. It can be done, but you will have to do some work, most of which will be emotionally painful.

Look back over your life and think of the labels and names people have called you. Some you may have brushed off, others still reside in your mind and heart.

Write down the labels and names and how they still impact your life. It is going to hurt and you may cry or even get angry. That's alright, but let's push through and take those negative names, labels and emotions to God in prayer, with a thankful heart, praising Him because of His faithfulness. As your prayers go up and you believe God's love, all the negative names and labels will fade away (Philippians 2: 9–11).

_____

_____

_____

_____

_____

Related topics: Chapter Three, I Am Valuable and Chapter Ten, Focus

CHAPTER NOTES

Here is your chance to write down a few thoughts of your own before we go to the next chapter.

_____

_____

_____

_____

_____

_____

_____

_____

_____

_____

_____

_____

_____

_____

_____

_____

_____

Chapter Five

Renew Me

Connecting the dots: Renewal doesn't just happen. First, you must submit your life to God on a daily basis.

Note 1: Everybody wants to change the world, yet nobody wants to do the hard work and renew their own minds by working on and correcting their personal issues that negatively impact them and everyone they come in contact with every day.

Note 2: Renewal occurs with a submission of our will, our weakness, and our faults to God. After years of living in denial, I did not want to see that I was weak. When I realized just how much God loved me, what He did by giving His Son to die for me, to think of me, and plan for me before I was even born, I realized I had no power unto myself. I submitted my problems to Him, and quickly realized that was not enough. I had to submit my life to Him, and I did. Submission comes first, then renewal. Renewal is a lifestyle. It is actively seeking the presence of God every day, all day. Renewal is changing the way you think, speak, hear, act, and respond. Submission to God's plan for your life is active. It is a day-by-day. process.

Note 3: Healing emotional wounds is a process. You can be healed, but you must also take what God has given you, His gift of forgiveness and freedom from condemnation (guilt, blaming yourself, believing that God can never love a person like you or forgive the things you have done). You can be healed and completely free. How? Read the Bible for yourself. Ask God to give you knowledge and wisdom. Pray throughout your day and ask the Holy Spirit to give you revelation and understanding. Then apply God's Word over and over again in your life (that means, take in God's Word personally and do what God says to do).

Note 4: Love and confusion cannot exist in the same space.

Note 5: People casually say, "Renew me Lord, take away the old me and make me new again" and "Yes, Lord, I will follow you. Make me like you" (that means, authenticate me). It has been my experience that new and mature Believers living a life of purpose; really don't understand what we are confessing. To do either, a person has to continually submit to renewing their mind, which I found to be painful and uncomfortable.

There is sadness and discomfort leaving people you care for and abandoning bad habits. On my journey, there has been a lot of crying and praying and depending on God to strengthen me and take care of every situation. But in the authentication process, there is also glorious love, healing, and freedom. The level of gratitude in acknowledging what God has done and released you from, instantaneously initiates unbounded praise and worship. In my opinion, it is the most freeing experience that a human can encounter; yet it is also a painful experience. Freedom is definitely not free.

Note 6: Some of the more trying days will be the days when you are challenged to renew your mind and step out of your old ways and step into the new person and purpose God originally intended for you. You can do it. Each day, situations will try you, but keep going. Read, study, pray, and meditate on God's Word and each day you will begin to witness the change in you.

Following are several Bible Scriptures to help support the renewing of your mind, transforming from the 'old" to the "new" person you were originally designed to be.

BIBLE SCRIPTURES

2 Corinthians 5:17 ESV, Therefore, if anyone is in Christ, he is a new creation. The old has passed away; behold, the new has come.

Colossians 3:10-12 ESV, And have put on the new self, which is being renewed in knowledge after the image of its creator. Here there is not Greek and Jew, circumcised and uncircumcised, barbarian, Scythian, slave, free; but Christ is all, and in all. Put on then, as God's chosen ones, holy and beloved, compassionate hearts, kindness, humility, meekness, and patience.

Romans 12:1–2 ESV, I appeal to you, therefore, brothers, by the mercies of God, to present your bodies as a living sacrifice, holy and acceptable to God, which is your spiritual worship. Do not be conformed to this world, but be transformed by the renewal of your mind, that by testing, you may discern what is the will of God, what is good and acceptable and perfect.

Psalm 51:10 ESV, Create in me a clean heart, O God, and renew a right spirit within me.

Psalm 147:3 ESV, He heals the brokenhearted and binds up their wounds.

APPLICATION

I write a lot about renewing your mind. What exactly does that mean? It means to replace evil thoughts with good and Godly thoughts; replacing bad habits with righteous habits. How do you exchange one thought for the other? I often tell people, for every personal issue you face, you have to do a mental exercise, meaning spend time reflecting on your personal issues and look back over your past to discover their causes. For example, a person who is a shopaholic spends too much money and runs themselves in debt. The Believers may say to the shopaholic, "Pray and be healed, give it to the Lord." But remember, with faith, work (action) is also required on our part. Dig a little deeper. The shopping and debt are personal issues—they are the symptoms of a deeper problem. Why does the shopaholic shop? Are they insecure, prideful, did they grow up in poverty? Do they seek assurance from others? What happened to them in their childhood or along the way of life? Who influenced them with this behavior, and they just do it because it is what they have always done? I don't have the answer, but whatever your personal issues are, they manifest in your everyday life.

Take some time to write down the personal issues you struggle with; take them to God; and pray for healing, knowledge, wisdom, discernment, and revelation. Do the mental exercise and think backward to the possible cause. In your revelation, you may discover that your past is actually ruling your present. God can and will heal you from every hurt, but it starts with you acknowledging that the hurt actually exists.

Related topics: Chapter One, Me and Chapter Twelve, Words Have Power

CHAPTER NOTES

Here is your chance to write down a few thoughts of your own before we go to the next chapter.

SECTION II: STANDING ON MY SQUARE

It takes a lot to navigate the daily dramas of life: personal issues, challenges, struggles, family, work, people. But I decided I was going to stand on my square and do what God told me to do: to tell people God loves them and that they are valuable and created for a purpose.

When you accept your purpose, you begin to realize the importance of what is required of you. It is easy to lose focus on your purpose when you are distracted with life and people who try their best to knock you off your square. As a Child of God, I am to show His Glory and not get tripped up in somebody's drama, but it happens. There were many days when I was knocked off my square, but I always got back up and re-centered (with prayer, revelation, correction, direction and study) because I believed that God had a plan and a purpose for my life much greater than any distraction or person.

Chapter Six

Purpose

Connecting the dots: God created us for a purpose; not our own, but His.

Note 1: Everyone has a purpose to discover. To be specific, this purpose, the reason God created you, is different than discovering or pursuing your personal desires and goals. In your purpose, the love of God and the job of spreading the message of Jesus Christ as our Lord and Savior is active as you walk, talk and reflect God's Glory. In living a life of purpose, you become that message of salvation that others can see.

Note 2: I was waiting for something big to happen; a huge event where God would reach down and tell me my purpose. I thought I only had to wait and He would make something extraordinary happen and tell me my assignment. Then I heard someone on the radio say, "Stop waiting on your miracle. God has already told you what to do; you just have to do it."

Those "big" moments are really small moments linked into one lifetime. "Small" moments occur each day I choose to surrender my life to Christ and act out my faith.

For me, small moments are living the life of a Believer. Saying good morning to God; adjusting my attitude with gratefulness; smiling at people as I walk by or enter an elevator; holding a door for someone; catching myself before I yell at my son, Elijah; being patient; giving someone the benefit of the doubt; catching my thoughts before jealousy sets in; focusing my thoughts on the presence of God; confessing my sins; saying I'm sorry; letting life flow; and thinking of me last. These are just a few of the small things I do, that linked together, demonstrates the Glory of God in my life. I am not to wait on the "big" things of life but to chase after the "small" moments of life. That is where God's Glory resides.

Note 3: I live a life of purpose. I know God loves me, which tells me I have value. He created me for a purpose. Because I love Him, I desire to do His will. For me, there is nothing more fulfilling than doing what God created me to do—to tell people that Jesus Christ is our Lord and Savior and that they have value and a purpose.

I wandered the earth for years wondering what am I here for? What should I do? And then, I finally discovered the reason for my existence: to praise Him and give Him all the Glory. Am I perfect? No. There are days when I fail but God, He gives mercy and grace and allows me to wake up the next day, get out of bed, and start all over again. I love being in God's presence. I love doing what God has called me to do.

I have heard it said that the most important day of your life is the day you were born. And that the second most important day is the "aha" moment when you discovered your purpose. In that "aha" moment, all things become new. "Therefore, if anyone is in Christ, he is a new creation. The old has passed away; behold, the new has come" (2 Corinthians 5:17).

Note 4: All of us have a purpose. Be careful in discerning what your talent is (what you are naturally good at doing) as opposed to your purpose—your spiritual gift(s)revealed by the Holy Spirit, in action, aligned with God's purpose and design for your life.

Following are several Bible Scriptures to help support the knowledge that you did not just happen, you were not a mistake; that God spent time thinking specifically about you, His Child, and how you fit strategically within His beautiful plans.

BIBLE SCRIPTURES

Jeremiah 29:11 ESV, For I know the plans I have for you, declares the Lord, plans for welfare and not for evil, to give you a future and a hope.

Ephesians 2:10 ESV, For we are His workmanship, created in Christ Jesus for good works, which God prepared beforehand, that we should walk in them.

Colossians 1:16 ESV, For by Him all things were created, in heaven and on earth, visible and invisible, whether thrones or dominions or rulers or authorities—all things were created through Him and for Him.

2 Timothy 1:9 ESV, Who saved us and called us to a holy calling, not because of our works but because of His own purpose and grace, which He gave us in Christ Jesus before the ages began.

Revelation 4:11 ESV, "Worthy are you, our Lord and God, to receive glory and honor and power, for you created all things, and by your will they existed and were created."

Ephesians 1:11 ESV, In Him we have obtained an inheritance, having been predestined according to the purpose of Him who works all things according to the counsel of His will.

Matthew 28: 16–20 ESV, Now the eleven disciples went to Galilee, to the mountain to which Jesus had directed them. And when they saw Him they worshiped Him, but some doubted. And Jesus came and said to them, "All authority in heaven and on earth has been given to me. Go therefore and make disciples of all nations, baptizing them in the name of the Father and of the Son and of the Holy Spirit, teaching them to observe all that I have commanded you. And behold, I am with you always, to the end of the age."

APPLICATION

The majority of people I talk with either don't know they have a purpose or are too afraid to receive their purpose. What if we all knew our purpose? Think about the people you interact with each day. What would your days look like if you and everyone you came in contact with knew their purpose?

Don't be afraid to receive and apply the Christian message of purpose in your life. Your application of God's Word to your life will definitely change you, but also how you interact with other people.

Have you discovered your purpose? Great. In one sentence, write your purpose below.

Don't know your purpose yet? No worries spend some time reading and studying the Biblical Scriptures above and then pray about it. The Holy Spirit will eventually tell you your purpose, but you will need to stay focused, with an open heart, so you can hear Him.

_____

_____

_____

_____

_____

_____

_____

Related topics: See Chapter Seven, The Power of Purpose and Appendix, Spiritual Gifts

CHAPTER NOTES

Here is your chance to write down a few thoughts of your own before we go to the next chapter.

_____

_____

_____

_____

_____

_____

_____

_____

_____

_____

_____

_____

_____

_____

_____

_____

_____

_____

Chapter Seven

The Power of Purpose

Connecting the dots: A life without PURPOSE is an aimless life.

Note 1: One of the best things about knowing my value and purpose is that I have a point of reference; a standard to return to when I fall short, get distracted, react to fear; or, even for a moment, hesitate to share my testimony. God gives me my own broad place (read Psalms 18:16-19) to return to and to continue my purpose.

Note 2: All of us have roles and responsibilities in this life. I am a woman, a mother, a wife, a friend, a sister, a daughter, and more. But our roles and responsibilities do not define us. Our Creator defines us to be a Child of God, a reflection of Him, a doer of His will.

Not long ago, I met a stranger who tried to tell me something negative about a good friend of mine; in essence, define my friend. They failed because my friend, Sue Simmers, walked in her purpose twenty-four hours a day, seven days a week as a missionary to thousands of people in Cameroon, Africa. I saw her help and care for people. I saw pictures of the Cameroonian schools, hospitals, and stores she helped build and the people she impacted simply by living a life of purpose.

People will try to define you—it's what we do. But our true value and purpose is defined by God. And when we consistently walk in our purpose, others can see clearly who we are: Children of God, reflections of Him, doers of His will and not our own.

Note 3: As Believers of Jesus Christ, we are not ultimately defined by our cumulative successes, failures, education, gender, finances, physical appearance, health, family and marital status, children, social media presence, or even our good works. As Believers, the true measure of our value and purpose will occur as stated in Matthew 25:23, when our Master says unto us, "Well done, good and faithful servant; thou has been faithful over a little; I will set you over much. Enter into the joy of your Master."

Note 4: When the creation asks why am I here, or why I was created, clearly, there is a disconnection from the Creator. That is why we all need to seek God and discover the purpose He has planned for our lives. Knowing your purpose connects you to God's plan.

Note 5: Living a life of purpose is a lifestyle. Many days you will be on target and in God's presence. Other days, you will be challenged spiritually. So what? Get back up, reset yourself, get back on your square, and do what you are supposed to be doing for God.

Note 6: The older I get, the more I notice the slight pains and inconvenience of getting older. But I thank God that He let me live this long to discover my purpose. There were countless days when He could have forgotten about me, but He gave me time and opportunities to finally realize and commit to His Plan for my life. It doesn't matter how old you are, God can still heal you and use you. We waste a lot of time in our youth chasing after what we want rather than chasing after God. Don't waste any more time. Answer God's call for your life and find out what He has for you to do. Don't wait or talk yourself out of it. Instead go to the Father, submit your will and ways to Him, and ask Him to show you your purpose.

Note 7: Your life is a story. Along the way, you have loved, you have lost, you have overcome, and you have learned many lessons. When you tell somebody about God as the main character in your story, your story now becomes your testimony and God now seems accessible to the listener. Your testimony has power and now the listener can see how God is applicable to their life as well. Go. Somebody is waiting for you to tell your testimony and be healed.

Following are several Bible Scriptures to help support the importance of aligning our lives to God's will.

BIBLE SCRIPTURES

Proverbs 19:21, ESV, Many are the plans in the mind of a man, but it is the purpose of the Lord that will stand.

Isaiah 43:7 ESV, Everyone who is called by my name, whom I created for my glory, whom I formed and made."

Jeremiah 1:5 ESV, "Before I formed you in the womb, I knew you, and before you were born I consecrated you; I appointed you a prophet to the nations."

John 15:16 ESV, You did not choose me, but I chose you and appointed you that you should go and bear fruit and that your fruit should abide, so that whatever you ask the Father in my name, He may give it to you.

1 Corinthians 6:19–20 ESV, Or do you not know that your body is a temple of the Holy Spirit within you, whom you have from God? You are not your own, for you were bought with a price. So glorify God in your body.

APPLICATION

When you are young, you think time will never end. When you get older, you realize your hourglass of sand is quickly slipping away. Know that as long as you are still breathing and in your right mind, you have time. Purpose is powerful. It shows up in ways you never conceived. When you start to learn to put God first instead of last, you will begin to see for yourself the power of purpose.

Purpose will:

- Open your heart and mind to new ideas and perspectives you never considered.

- Make you happier and content with your position in life.

- Draw out your weaknesses and identify the spiritual gifts you have denied or ignored your whole life.

- Make you work harder than you ever worked before, but you don't care, because the joy and completeness you receive from pleasing God is more than you could have ever imagined.

- Motivate and keep you focused.

Related topic: Chapter Six, Purpose and Appendix, Spiritual Gifts

CHAPTER NOTES

Here is your chance to write down a few thoughts of your own before we go to the next chapter.

_____

_____

_____

_____

_____

_____

_____

_____

_____

_____

_____

_____

_____

_____

_____

_____

_____

_____

_____

Chapter Eight

Conform

Connecting the dots: We, as Children of God, are to influence the world–not the other way around.

Note 1: Some of us have a face we show the world, another face we show to family and friends, and maybe even another face when we are alone. Who are you, really? Do you know? God calls us to our individual purpose, so we are His alone. We are not to conform to this world, but we are to walk in our purpose daily so that others will witness God's salvation in our lives and believe that God will do the same for them.

Note 2: Sometimes life is simply black or white. Right or left. Good or evil. Thank God for His Word, His love, His strength, and His mercy—all of which give us a solid foundation, a point of reference, a square to stand on, a faith to hold onto, a value to maintain, a plan to look forward to, and a purpose to complete. This world can be evil and confusing. It can take a lot to navigate the daily drama of life. Sometimes, we get hit with more than we think we can handle. And sometimes, we may think, life would be easier if we just gave up and acted like the world. But we know in our hearts that can never be. It was just the devil testing our resolve. I know it's hard, but Jesus never said it would be easy; so, I press on. I am not going backwards. I am not going to conform to the world. And I am not abandoning my faith. I am not going to be anybody but who I was called to be, a Child of God. So, my only choice is to stand on my square and not be moved.

Note 3: A popular phrase these days is "be your authentic self" which has nothing to do with the "authentic you" that is a one-of-a-kind, beautiful creation of God. There has never been anyone else exactly like you. Never. So, if you want to do something meaningful, important, and out of the ordinary that will impact the world, your community, your family and friends, and even you, then be the "authentic you" God created you to be.

Note 4: Be careful. The more time we spend entangled in fear, doubt, distractions, bitterness, and drama, the less time we spend with God and the further we drift away from our true purpose. Those little rationalized compromises here and there eventually take hold and chip away at our peace, faith, and conviction. So, be alert and discern your own heart because Satan comes to seek and destroy, and often it occurs in subtle and small ways.

Following are several Bible Scriptures to help you stay focused and not conform to the world's standards As Believers; we should live in such a way that people see God's Glory in us and are drawn to know more about Him.

BIBLE SCRIPTURES

Romans 12:2 ESV, Do not be conformed to this world, but be transformed by the renewal of your mind, that by testing you may discern what is the will of God, what is good and acceptable and perfect.

Romans 8:29 ESV, For those whom He foreknew He also predestined to be conformed to the image of His Son, in order that He might be the firstborn among many brothers.

Ecclesiastes 1:9 ESV, What has been is what will be, and what has been done is what will be done, and there is nothing new under the sun.

John 10:10 ESV, The thief comes only to steal and kill and destroy. I came that they may have life and have it abundantly.

Ezekiel 11:12 ESV, And you shall know that I am the LORD. For you have not walked in my statutes, nor obeyed my rules, but have acted according to the rules of the nations that are around you.

APPLICATION

When I teach purpose classes, as an example, I like to use a white robe covered with my personal issues: pride, jealousy, envy, fear, etc. Believe me, there are more, but you get the point. Now, in your mind, picture your own white robe covered with your personal issues.

I want you to consider what happens when we are wearing our white robes with our personal issues and we meet other people. What happens when there is a disagreement? What happens when we get married? What happens when we have children? What happens in our jobs and businesses?

Answer: chaos, anger, harsh words, misunderstandings, divorce, abuse, even loss of life. Some of us don't want to take off our marked-up white robes because they are comfortable and we think *this is who I am*. But really, how has that been working for you? I know all about it. I am the queen of denial ... but you have to start somewhere. If you want better, you have to do better.

For me, there is nothing as sad as listening to someone passionately tell me why they have to continue to wear their marked-up white robe. The same robe that steals their joy and keeps them bound and powerless. Believe me, a better life is on the other side of your pain but first you will need to submit your personal issues and then your life to God and allow Him to heal you.

It's time for you to be fearless and list your personal issues. Then, right next to each issue, in one sentence state how you allowed the issue to negatively impact someone this past week.

Here is an example for you to follow:

Personal issue: *Pride. This week at work, I was having a conversation with a coworker regarding an important issue and because I felt I was right and should be heard, I kept interrupting them.* Now, it's your turn.

#1 Personal issue: _____

#2 Personal issue:_____

#3 Personal issue: _____

In the process of living a life of purpose, you can't choose to let God heal one or two personal issues and decide to keep a few on the side because you are too afraid to deal with them. Purpose does not work that way, God will continually test you on your weakness over and over again until you learn the lesson. For me it took years to make the connections. Your personal issues are simply your weakness Satan uses to keep you bound and conformed to the world. So for each of your personal issues (weaknesses) you have to go to the Bible and study them. My #1 personal issue was emotional neglect which manifested in pride. Again, I Googled "Bible scriptures pride" learned how this emotion had impacted every area of my life. Through applying God's Word concerning pride over my life I learned this was a tactic Satan used over and over (in different scenarios with different people) that kept me unhappy the majority of my life even through what the world would consider a "successful" life and career. So be fearless, write down your personal issues and discover your weaknesses.

Related topics: Chapter Four, I Know Who I Am and Chapter Thirteen, Be Better

CHAPTER NOTES

Here is your chance to write down a few thoughts of your own before we go to the next chapter.

_____

_____

_____

_____

_____

_____

_____

_____

_____

_____

_____

_____

_____

_____

_____

_____

_____

_____

Chapter Nine

Fear

Connecting the dots: **Some of us know we need to change our lives, but we don't want to put in the effort. Some of us are afraid to learn more than what we already know. Some of us are in denial. And some of us simply refuse to change.**

Note 1: Fear is the #1 obstacle holding you back from more love, peace, joy, and all the promises God has for you. Fear is holding you back from healing (emotionally and physically). Fear is holding you back from forgiveness. Fear is holding you back from meeting the "authentic you" God named and planned for ages ago. Fear is not from God. There is power in you.

Note 2: Fearful = a person who is afraid, not sure, cautious, doubting, second-guessing God's Word even though they know God has called them to a purpose. A fearful person believes the excuses they play over and over again in their thoughts.

Fearless = a person who answers God's calls for their life, knows God has a purpose and a plan for their life, and is committed to obeying God. They know there will be obstacles, challenges, heartache, pain, sacrifices, criticism, and time away from family and friends. But they also know they will walk in faith through every door and every opportunity God provides them. They do not operate out of fear, but out of love and reverence to God. Being fearless doesn't just happen, it's a process. Initially it's painful and feels like you are stepping off a cliff. But then as you take the first steps toward purpose you will discover unimaginable peace and gratitude that God would choose you to participate in His plan. The more I learn about God's love and purpose for my life, the more fearless and bolder I become.

Note 3: Which person are you most afraid of? The person you are or the person you will be when you finally answer God's call? Get over your fear and discover the purpose God has designed specifically for you.

Note 4: Oh, taste and see that the Lord is good Blessed is the man who takes refuge in Him!, (Psalm 34:8) I recently spoke with a broken person who has discovered their spiritual gift. Now they are at a crossroad. They have tasted just a portion of His Glory and they now have to make a decision of which road to travel.

Will they continue on the road on the left that they know—fear, self-doubt, regret, and a broken heart? This road is not always comfortable but they know it and what to expect. Or, will they be fearless and choose the new road on the right, that will heal their broken heart? This road has never been traveled, but they know it leads to healing because they have seen others on this road; they have tasted God's Glory, been touched by His presence, and know there is more to experience on the road to the right.

I pray that every broken spirit remembers their moment in the presence of God and that they choose another taste, and another, until they are filled with the one true love, the love of God that can heal every broken heart.

Note 5: There is a strong correlation between what you will do for someone you know versus someone you don't know. The same thing applies to your relationship with God. The more you know about Him, the more you will want to do for Him—including discovering your value and purpose. Stop being afraid. There is no danger in getting to know more about God.

Note 6: Follow Him. One of our greatest fears is losing. We think we are the center of the world and everything we have is because of our own efforts. Not so. God, through His love, mercy, and grace gave you a job, a home, a car, food, clothes, and all that you have. God gave you life, health, strength, and time—not because you are so good, but because He chooses to bless you. Give up the idea that your life is your own—because, it is not. Your life belongs to God. And stop being afraid to answer His call and follow Him. Stop being afraid of what you believe you will lose. Because, guess what? It was never yours to begin with.

Following are several Bible Scriptures to help strengthen you along your journey of purpose.

BIBLE SCRIPTURES

Philippians 4:6 ESV, Do not be anxious about anything, but in everything by prayer and supplication with thanksgiving, let your requests be made known to God.

Philippians 4:13 ESV, I can do all things through Him who strengthens me.

2 Timothy 1:7 ESV, For God gave us a spirit not of fear but of power and love and self-control.

Isaiah 54:17 ESV, No weapon that is fashioned against you shall succeed and you shall confute every tongue that rises against you in judgment. This is the heritage of the servants of the Lord and their vindication from me, declares the Lord.

Isaiah 43:1–3 ESV, But now thus says the Lord, He who created you, O Jacob, He who formed you, O Israel: "Fear not, for I have redeemed you; I have called you by name, you are mine. When you pass through the waters, I will be with you; and through the rivers, they shall not overwhelm you; when you walk through fire you shall not be burned, and the flame shall not consume you. For I am the Lord your God, the Holy One of Israel, your Savior. I give Egypt as your ransom, Cush and Seba in exchange for you."

1 John 4:18 ESV, There is no fear in love, but perfect love casts out fear. For fear has to do with punishment, and who-ever fears has not been perfected in love.

Psalm 27:1–5 ESV, The Lord is my light and my salvation; whom shall I fear? The Lord is the stronghold of my life; of whom shall I be afraid? When evildoers assail me to eat up my flesh, my adversaries and foes, it is they who stumble and fall. Though an army encamp against me, my heart shall not fear; though war arise against me, yet I will be confident. One thing have I asked of the Lord, that will I seek after: that I may dwell in the house of the Lord all the days of my life, to gaze upon the beauty of the Lord and to inquire in His temple. For He will hide me in His shelter in the day of trouble; He will conceal me under the cover of His tent; He will lift me high upon a rock.

Psalm 34:4 ESV, I sought the Lord, and He answered me and delivered me from all my fears.

Psalm 37:1–5 ESV, Of David. Fret not yourself because of evildoers; be not envious of wrongdoers! For they will soon fade like the grass and wither like the green herb. Trust in the Lord, and do good; dwell in the land and befriend faithfulness. Delight yourself in the Lord, and He will give you the desires of your heart. Commit your way to the Lord; trust in Him, and He will act.

Psalm 56:3–4 ESV, When I am afraid, I put my trust in you. In God, whose word I praise, in God I trust; I shall not be afraid. What can flesh do to me?

Romans 8:15 ESV, For you did not receive the spirit of slavery to fall back into fear, but you have received the Spirit of adoption as sons, by whom we cry, "Abba! Father!"

Romans 8:31 ESV, What then shall we say to these things? If God is for us, who can be against us?

Romans 8:38–39 ESV, For I am sure that neither death nor life, nor angels nor rulers, nor things present nor things to come, nor powers, nor height nor depth, nor anything else in all creation, will be able to separate us from the love of God in Christ Jesus our Lord.

APPLICATION

What is it that stops us from answering the small, still voice of God which beckons us to get to know Him better? What in our lives draws our attention and causes us to ignore His voice and choose to hide instead? What is better than God, that we choose not to answer Him? What hurt do we carry that causes us to rationalize that we are not good enough or have sinned so much that we cannot be forgiven? The biggest obstacle in our lives is fear, which is not always obvious.

Two agents of fear we may not easily recognize are procrastination and insecurity. Sometimes you do something for so long, you don't even realize you are doing it. Procrastinators intently state they are going to do something, but they don't. They tend to overthink and never reach a conclusion. Insecure people are always wondering if someone likes them; are afraid to have their own opinions; or think they are not good enough, too old, too young, too short, too tall, too poor, too fat, too skinny, uneducated, too dark, too light, too something.

If any of this sounds like you, please recognize it for what it is—fear. Take some time and do the mental exercise and think back over your life and try to figure out why you procrastinate and/or are insecure and challenge yourself to reset those old emotions of fear.

How do you reset your emotions? Google "Bible verses on God's love." Then read, study, and apply God's Word and you will begin to see what God sees in you—a beautiful creation, wonderfully made, able to do all things through Jesus Christ. It's time to walk through your host of enemies (fear), prepare yourself for God's promises, and possess the land (see and take what God has given you).

I challenge you to answer these questions for yourself. Answering God's voice and call for your life will lead you to God's unlimited love and ultimately to discovering God's purpose for your life.

I think my biggest fear is not being in control, but God has definitely been testing me on that and showing me how to let go and have faith in Him, and also how to have faith in myself.

What are you afraid of? Below is space for you to list three of your biggest fears. Then write down why you believe you have these fears. Follow my example:

Example: *My fear: Not being in control. Why? Emotional neglect as a child caused me to be insecure. My response (symptoms) are over checking things and anger.*

#1 Fear: _____

Why?_____

My Response:_____

#1 Fear: _____

Why?_____

My Response:_____

#1 Fear: _____

Why?_____

My Response:_____

Now, go back and study the Bible scriptures for this chapter and apply over your life.

Related topics: Chapter Fourteen, Struggles and Chapter Twenty, Forgiveness

CHAPTER NOTES

Here is your chance to write down a few thoughts of your own before we go to the next chapter.

Chapter Ten

Focus

Connecting the dots: It has been a long journey, yet I still know whose I am, what I am, and what I am here to do. Stay focused and stay blessed.

Note 1: It's easy to get comfortable. Keep your eyes and ears open for the one that comes to destroy you. Stay faithful, focused, diligent, and in prayer; and protect the purpose that God has given you to complete.

Note 2: You can't be in everybody's business and in God's presence at the same time. You just can't.

Note 3: Day-to-day life can take a toll on us—especially when manufactured drama is involved. We can easily get caught up, lose our focus; and get stressed, bitter, angry, or depressed. We must remember that we always have a choice in our responses. Proverbs 12:25 says, "Anxiety in the heart of man causes depression, but a good word maketh it glad." Speak positive words to yourself and over your situation. Know that everything will be all right and choose to be happy and enjoy this day that the Lord has made.

Note 4: Instead of swinging at every issue, instead of defending my position and being mad and frustrated, instead of letting bitterness and discontent sink in, I realize that I need to listen to God and trust Him.

Following are several Bible Scriptures to help you stay focused on your journey of living a life of purpose.

BIBLE SCRIPTURES

Matthew 6:33 ESV, But seek first the kingdom of God and His righteousness, and all these things will be added to you.

Genesis 4:6–7 ESV, The Lord said to Cain, "Why are you angry, and why has your face fallen? If you do well, will you not be accepted? And if you do not do well, sin is crouching at the door. Its desire is for you, but you must rule over it."

1 Corinthians 10:13 ESV, No temptation has overtaken you that is not common to man. God is faithful and He will not let you be tempted beyond your ability, but with the temptation He will also provide the way of escape, that you may be able to endure it.

Romans 5:3–5 ESV, Not only that, but we rejoice in our sufferings, knowing that suffering produces endurance, and endurance produces character, and character produces hope, and hope does not put us to shame, because God's love has been poured into our hearts through the Holy Spirit who has been given to us.

APPLICATION

You need to have a strong mind that continually seeks the presence of God in order to walk through your life challenges and struggles. Recognize that the devil comes to steal your joy, your peace, your love, your faith, and your purpose. Stay focused on God's Word and all the lessons you have learned so far in your journey as a Believer, and hold your ground.

We live in a culture that bombards us with information and news, from the time we get up in the morning until we go to sleep at night. Add the typical responsibilities of caring for our families, going to work, running errands, and going to school, and we can easily get distracted and lose our focus.

I start my days by thanking God for the day ahead and marinating myself in praise and worship music as I get ready for work; often listening to Bishop TD Jakes on my way to work, courtesy of YouTube. I encourage you to find and implement your own way of starting your day focused on God.

Below, briefly write down how you stay focused or what you intend to implement to help you stay focused.

_____

_____

_____

_____

_____

Related topic: Chapter Eight, Conform

CHAPTER NOTES

Here is your chance to write down a few thoughts of your own before we go to the next chapter.

Chapter Eleven

Our Relationship with God

oⅈⅈⅈ~ ~ⅈⅈⅈo

Connecting the dots: You might think otherwise, but we need God for everything. Yes, everything.

Note 1: The simple fact that you woke up this morning is confirmation of God speaking to you. Now, what will you say to God?

Note 2: Sometimes we get lax in our relationship with God. That is a big problem because we leave ourselves open to repeating the same lessons over and over again. When we think I got this, we soon find out we are not good at fighting the devil. This time, I am staying close to God so He can fight my battles. He told me to trust Him—and I will.

Note 3: The closer you get to understanding your value and purpose, the more you will realize it is not about you, it is about God and what He wants you to do.

Following are several Bible Scriptures to help support the importance of maintaining a righteous relationship with God. Just like any relationship, you need to spend time together to get to know His character, likes, dislikes and His plan for your life.

BIBLE SCRIPTURES

Genesis 1:26–28 ESV, Then God said, "Let us make man in our image, after our likeness. And let them have dominion over the fish of the sea and over the birds of the heavens and over the livestock and over all the earth and over every creeping thing that creeps on the earth." So God created man in His own image, in the image of God He created him; male and female He created them. And God blessed them. And God said to them, "Be fruitful and multiply and fill the earth and subdue it, and have dominion over the fish of the sea and over the birds of the heavens and over every living thing that moves on the earth."

1 Samuel 12:24 ESV, Only fear the LORD and serve Him in truth with all your heart; for consider what great things He has done for you.

Psalm 111:10 ESV, The fear of the Lord is the beginning of wisdom; all those who practice it have a good understanding. His praise endures forever!

John 4:24 ESV, God is spirit and those who worship Him must worship in spirit and truth."

APPLICATION

Relationships are established with time, communication, emotion, and commitment. When you immediately open your eyes in the morning, start your dialog with God by thanking Him for waking you up to a brand-new day.

Then acknowledge God's sovereignty and thank Him for all He has done, including His friendship, faithfulness, goodness, mercy, and favor.

You might say, "Well, I don't hear God speaking to me" or "He doesn't talk to me anymore." God is continually talking to you, the problem is are you hearing what He is saying? He is communicating to you every day when He puts breath in your body, when He wakes you up, when you walk into the kitchen and make breakfast, when you commute to work and when you return, when you show and receive love and in other countless ways.

The problem is, you do not realize your value. So you naively choose to believe the lies Satan and social media offer as distractions instead of choosing the truth God proclaims. God has been talking to you through His faithfulness, His Word, and His Son, Jesus Christ, your entire life. The question is: Are you taking the time to listen to God and communicate with Him? Purpose starts with a relationship with God. The more you find out how God feels about you, the more you will fall in love with Him.

Please find and read Psalms 139:13–18 on a Study Bible and let it sink in for a bit. You were custom designed ages ago and you were never a mistake.

continued on next page

After reading Psalm 139:13-18, I want you to write down three things you can and will do every day to strengthen your relationship with God.

1._____

2._____

3._____

Related topics: Chapter Sixteen, Prayer and Meditation and Chapter Nineteen, Faithfulness

CHAPTER NOTES

Here is your chance to write down a few thoughts of your own before we go to the next chapter.

_____

_____

_____

_____

_____

_____

_____

_____

_____

_____

_____

_____

_____

_____

_____

_____

_____

_____

_____

Chapter Twelve

Words Have Power

Connecting the dots: My spiritual growth, and even my decline, are impacted by the words I speak.

Note 1: One of the most beautiful words you can say (in any language)—a word that is powerful, liberating, and requires no reasoning—is NO. I realize it might be difficult for you to say NO to people, and it may take practice, but you can do it. You can learn to say the word. Say NO to people who use and drain you. Say NO to your full calendar, that has you running with no rest. Say NO to the person who thinks your money and time is their own. Say NO to anybody who abuses you. Say NO to anybody who tries to belittle and devalue you. As I said, NO is a beautiful and liberating word. Getting rid of the distractions and drama in your life will create time for the most important thing: your relationship with God.

Note 2: When I stop listening to myself, the little girl in me looking for love and attention, I will have the capacity to hear what God has to say about me, my value, and my purpose.

Note 3: The more I speak about a negative situation, the more powerful and real it becomes in my mind and my space.

Note 4: Stop telling your enemies how you feel. This is how they plan against you. Instead, tell God how you feel. He will fight your battles and win each and every one.

Note 5: There are some words you can't take back and some actions you can't do over; So, instead, love to the best of your abilities.

Note 6: I am convinced that if we think, speak, and do more that is good, kind, patient, and positive the world will do the same. Don't be fooled. Light will always conquer darkness.

Following are several Bible Scriptures to help you realize the power words have. Mark 11:23 tells us that faith combined with words can move mountains.

BIBLE SCRIPTURES

Ephesians 4:29 ESV, Let no corrupting talk come out of your mouths, but only such as is good for building up, as fits the occasion, that it may give grace to those who hear.

Matthew 12:36 ESV, I tell you, on the day of judgment, people will give account for every careless word they speak.

Mark 11:23 ESV, Truly, I say to you, whosoever says to this mountain, "Be taken up and thrown in the sea, and does not doubt in his heart, but believes what He says will come to pass, it will be done for him."

Proverbs 15:1 ESV, A soft answer turns away wrath, but a harsh word stirs up anger.

Proverbs 15:4 ESV, A gentle tongue is a tree of life, but perverseness in it breaks the spirit.

Matthew 15:18 ESV, But what comes out of the mouth proceeds from the heart, and this defiles a person.

Colossians 3:8 ESV, But now you must put them all away: anger, wrath, malice, slander, and obscene talk from your mouth.

Colossians 4:6 ESV, Let your speech always be gracious, seasoned with salt, so that you may know how you ought to answer each person.

APPLICATION

Throughout your life, people have called you names, labeled you, and told you what you cannot do—which has negatively impacted you. And, during your life, you have done the same to others. Negative words build negative people. Good and Godly words build good and Godly people.

We often hear the phrase "You are what you eat." I also believe we are what we hear.

I challenge you to start new habits. Start your day by speaking to God in prayer, and during the day, when you catch yourself thinking or saying something negative about yourself, cross that out and tell yourself the opposite. God has already told us what He feels about us in the Bible, the problem is that we need to start believing what we read and speaking God's word over our lives to change the atmosphere.

Below, write down three negative things you catch yourself thinking or saying about yourself or others, and then next to it write down a positive affirmation. Follow my example:

Example: I'm too old to start a new business. / You are never too old to try new things and experiences, including starting a business.

1._____

2._____

3._____

Related topics: Chapter Fifteen, Bitterness and
Chapter Seventeen, Meekness

CHAPTER NOTES

Here is your chance to write down a few thoughts of your own before we go to the next chapter.

_____

_____

_____

_____

_____

_____

_____

_____

_____

_____

_____

_____

_____

_____

_____

_____

SECTION III: FOLLOW HIM

In this stage of my life, I was going through a series of challenges and struggles orchestrated by a manipulating coworker that lasted about eighteen months. About a year into this period at work, I realized that the change and conflicts I was experiencing were actually a lesson that I kept failing because of my weakness—pride. I now know the challenges and struggles were lessons to prepare me for what God called me to do—my purpose. But first, I had to learn the lessons and walk through each challenge and struggle with Jesus Christ, our Lord and Savior, as my model and teacher.

This eighteen-month period was full of change, bitterness, jealousy, fear, and anger and eventually healing and forgiveness. My fall from pride took me to my core, and I finally began to realize I was nothing without God, and in another sense, everything to Him. As I wrote this book, I realized that Chapter 15, Struggles, would be the longest chapter.

The challenges and struggles we go through, if we learn and respond righteously, should be catalysts to our spiritual growth. Each challenge and struggle I experienced was necessary to help me trust God—but those experiences also healed me and liberated me from my weakness of pride. I still work at the same place and while some things have changed for the better, the biggest and best change has occurred in me and how I respond.

I thank God for the lesson, which tested me and authenticated what I believe, that I am a Child of God living a life of purpose. It is easy to say the words, "Lord I will follow you." I learned it was so much harder to actually do when I was trying to lead. Jesus should be in front, leading as our model and teacher, and we should be in the back, following as servants.

Chapter Thirteen

Be Better

Connecting the dots: We all have the capacity to be and do better. Including me.

Note 1: I was a bit agitated the other day and I found myself listening to Brinda rather than choosing to listen to the Holy Spirit. But, I soon remembered my Bible study on wisdom. I quickly picked up my Bible and read Proverbs 16 where the bulk of my problems were addressed and I began to feel better. One Scripture that said so much to me was: Proverbs 16:7, "When a man's ways please the Lord, He maketh even his enemies be at peace with him." Today, less of me Lord, more of you.

Note 2: Oftentimes we allow ourselves to get into personal ruts. Eating the same food, wearing the same colors, driving the same route to work, thinking the same negative thoughts; even saying the same prayer over and over. And, as we go along day by day, we think we are "good"—and maybe we are. But what about being "better"? Each day, I have to challenge myself to be better; to smile more, to think and act as a Child of God, to listen more and talk less, to be patient and not complain, to change my expectations, to do better than I did yesterday. Is it hard? Yes. Do

I ever fail? Yes. Do I keep going? Yes. It is easy to be "good" and even average. My daily goal is to continually work at being better.

Note 3: Some people have a rebellious spirit and don't want anybody telling them what to do—even the message of discovering their value and purpose. I understand that spirit and I still struggle with my own rebellious mindset. From time to time, I have to check myself and get back in line with God's Word. Be careful. A rebellious mind is not from God.

Note 4: I am so happy to be free; so happy to give all my cares, doubts, and fears to my God. He listens to me. He is patient with me. He corrects and directs me. He disciplines and heals me. He takes every tear and turns it into a lesson. I wait on Him, for His will to be done. No complaining, no pride, no resentment is acceptable. I slow down so I can hear Him. And, I pray for strength to press on so that I can learn the lesson; to be meek and lowly in spirit; to hold my peace, be still and let God do His will. Surely, victory is on the other side. It feels so good to be free.

Following are several Bible Scriptures to help encourage you to seek after the abundant (better) life God promises us as we align ourselves to His will.

BIBLE SCRIPTURES

Philippians 4:8 ESV, Finally, brothers, whatever is true, whatever is honorable, whatever is just, whatever is pure, whatever is lovely, whatever is commendable, if there is any excellence, if there is anything worthy of praise, think about these things.

Ephesians 5:20 ESV, Giving thanks always and for everything to God the Father in the name of our Lord Jesus Christ.

Romans 8:28 ESV, And we know that for those who love God, all things work together for good, for those who are called according to His purpose.

John 10:10 ESV, The thief comes only to steal and kill and destroy. I came that they may have life and have it abundantly.

Jeremiah 29:11 ESV, For I know the plans I have for you, declares the Lord, plans for welfare and not for evil, to give you a future and a hope.

APPLICATION

Regardless of our positions in life, we all have room for improvement, we all can do better, we all can be open to thinking beyond our typical everyday thoughts and learning and experiencing more.

Getting older? Me too. So what? The end is not here yet and there is still time to learn, to try new things, meet new people, and open our mind and heart to new perspectives. And don't just rely on what you hear. Check, dissect, and discern the information you take in; particularly when it comes to God's Word. Tidbits of Bible verses on Facebook and Instagram are not Bible study. Carve out some time in your day and read and study the Bible for yourself. You don't have to be perfect, but you can be better.

Sometimes we are afraid to try something new for fear of stretching beyond our comfort level. Think about three things you have thought about doing but never did. Write them down below and then plan on doing them. Trying these new experiences will help push you out of your everyday box and, in turn, open and give you new perspectives and life experiences.

1._____

2. _____

3. _____

Related topics: Chapter Five, Renew Me and
Chapter Twelve, Words Have Power

CHAPTER NOTES

Here is your chance to write down a few thoughts of your own before we go to the next chapter.

_____

_____

_____

_____

_____

_____

_____

_____

_____

_____

_____

_____

_____

_____

_____

_____

_____

_____

_____

_____

Chapter Fourteen

Struggles

Connecting the dots: Struggles introduce us to our weaknesses. In each struggle, there is a lesson not yet mastered.

Note 1: "Take my yoke upon you, and learn from me, for I am gentle and lowly in heart, and you will find rest for your souls" (Matthew 11:29). I discovered that once I encounter a challenge or struggle, I should focus less on the events occurring outside of me and more on what should be happening inside of me. First, I need to activate my faith. Next, I need to think back on a past challenge or struggle and consider what the Holy Spirit is revealing to me. Third, I need to put Jesus in front of me and follow His examples of being humble, meek, and obedient. Jesus accepted His purpose and was arrested, accused, beaten, judged, and finally led to the cross and killed. His humility, patience, and total submission of His will to that of the Father is our example of meekness. So, I need to be quiet, not complain or argue, but press through to my victory, confident that God is in control. I can change my life, my experience, and my emotions by changing my expectations and aligning myself to God's will.

Note 2: Yesterday I felt pushed to the edge of my square. This morning, I found comfort in Psalm 31:15: "My times are in your hands; deliver me from the hands of my enemies, from those who pursue me." I copied Psalm 31 and will keep it close to me today. I must stay mindful that spiritual warfare is at play. But, more importantly, that God is my strength and that joy is definitely on the other side.

Note 3: Last week, I thought: it's illogical for a logical person to try to have a logical conversation with an illogical person. Then, my thoughts shifted spiritually and I knew a spiritual person focused on God will not have much success trying to communicate with a person focused on the world and its desires. And such is the problem: people on two different sides.

While reading 1 John 4, I focused on verses 4-6. I can talk until I pass out. I can try to convince someone to my side. I can stress myself out trying to figure out how to convey my heart, it will not matter. If we are not on the same side, they will not understand what I am saying and I will not understand them because their ideas, agenda, and perception of me come from the world and not from God. So, I will trust God. I will shift my conversations to Him and wait on the victory He has already promised.

"Beloved, do not believe every spirit, but test the spirits to see whether they are from God, for many false prophets have gone out into the world. By this, you know the Spirit of God: every spirit that confesses that Jesus Christ has come in the flesh is from God, and every spirit that does not confess Jesus is not from God. This is the spirit of the antichrist, which you heard was coming and now is in the world already. Little children, you are from God and have overcome them, for he who is in you is greater than he who is in the world. They are from the world; therefore they speak from the world, and the world listens to them. We are from God. Whoever knows God listens to us; whoever is not from God does not listen to us. By this, we know the Spirit of truth and the spirit of error" (1 John 4:1-6).

Note 4: When we go through challenges and struggles and come out on the other side victorious, we gain revelations, learn about our weaknesses and sins, and our faith in God should grow stronger. Be careful and don't forget what the Holy Spirit has taught you. Keep the knowledge and wisdom you gained while walking in the valley in front of you as a reminder. Meditate on it, hold it close, and remember to apply what the Holy Spirit taught you in similar situations. I don't want to keep repeating the same lesson plan. I want to graduate and move up to the next level God is preparing me for.

Note 5: As I journey in my struggle, I am an easy target for spiritual warfare and vexation. Vexation is the agitation and strife that lingers in the midst of a struggle. Yesterday, I started my day with good intentions, but failed to listen to the Holy Spirit and realize trouble was on the horizon. So today, I am going to do better. I will listen to the Holy Sprint and take more mental notes. I thought the lesson from this struggle was over, but I see I have more to learn.

Note 6: As I walk this life of purpose, it seems there is more coming at me than ever before. But God provides for me through His Word, "I consider that our present sufferings are not worth comparing with the glory that will be revealed in us" (Romans 8:18). This passage is full of wisdom and direction. When I am tired or afraid I can ask God for help. God hears me, but I must be patient in the midst of my struggles. The hope I have in God outweighs the struggle.

Note 7: Yesterday was a good day. People can say there is no God, but it's amazing that you can pick up your Bible, read God's Word and be healed or be drawn to a scripture that provides comfort, direction, and even correction. Romans 5:3-5 says, "Not only so, but we also glory in our sufferings, because we know that suffering produces perseverance; perseverance, character;

and character, hope. And hope does not put us to shame, because God's love has been poured out into our hearts through the Holy Spirit who has been given to us." Personally, I don't like to suffer, but it's necessary. It's easy for me to praise God and be good and act right when I feel my life is all good. But when I am going through a struggle, my true character and weaknesses will soon be revealed. In the larger text of Romans 5:1-11, I have gleaned the following: The more struggles I go through, the more I realize I need to depend on God. Depending on Him requires patience; and along the way, that patience shapes my character. I get a bit bruised as I am being reshaped, but I know that on the other side there is hope and God's love, which truly outweighs and conquers any struggle I go through. As always, God has already worked it out. So, even when I am going through a struggle, I must remember to praise God. My praise is a reflection of my character.

Note 8: Lately, there has been so much change going on in my life. I am reminded in Ecclesiastics 1:9-11 that what is new to me is really not new at all, but is the continuation of life—including the drama that follows. "What has been will be again, what has been done will be done again; there is nothing new under the sun. Is there anything of which one can say, 'Look! This is something new'? It was here already, long ago; it was here before our time. No one remembers the former generations, and even those yet to come will not be remembered by those who follow them" (Ecclesiastics 1:9-11). Stay focused on God and His Word and His Way. The battle is already won. God's will—it will be done regardless of what the world says or does.

Note 9: Change is happening everywhere—some good; some not so good. Change happens at work, in our families and in our children, in our bodies, in our marriages, and sometimes in our finances. I am human, so when not-so-good change occurs, my mood changes. I had to remind myself this morning that in those moments of uncertainty, Romans 8:28 KJV is still true: "And we know that all things work together for good to them that love God, to them who are called according to His purpose." Change comes, goes, and comes back again. That is life. I must remain confident that God is in control (of me, the world, the universe) and that everything (me, the world, the universe) will work out the way He planned it and the results will be good.

Note 10: When I ask God to fight my battles, I know He will take care of them. So I remind myself to smile through difficult moments and be patient. My prayers will be answered. The victory is already won, all I have to do is stay faithful and stay righteous.

Note 11: My flesh says yes, but God's Word speaks to my spirit to prepare. Go and put on your salvation, the truth, faith, righteousness, and peace. God will handle this fight.

Note 12: Yesterday, I could have been a lot better. I found myself agitated by people at work who lie and manipulate to push their personal agendas all the while unconcerned how their actions hurt other people. I woke up this morning feeling guilty, thinking about how I allowed my weaknesses to control my response over and over again. This morning, I asked the Lord for a topic to study and I was given "my grace is sufficient." In 2 Corinthians 12:9, God tells the Apostle Paul that, "His grace is sufficient for thee: for my strength is made perfect in weakness." I asked the Lord to forgive me, and I am not going to beat myself up about it. My weakness gives me the opportunity to see that I cannot do anything without God. God gives us grace because we are not strong enough to deal with the world alone. I need Him in every situation, including dealing with people and situations that agitate me. I am thankful that I have a loving God who gives me another day of grace to learn and to do better.

Note 13: Believing and speaking out loud on what I believe may not shorten my struggle, but it does change my perspective. (2 Corinthians 4:13) .

Note 14: I am not certain what season I am going through, but I do know I need an abundance of God's Word to be what He wants me to be. He said, "Trust Him" and I will. For those of us struggling to find peace, 2 Corinthians 4:16-18 says: "Therefore we do not lose heart. Though outwardly we are wasting away, yet inwardly we are being renewed day by day. For our light and momentary troubles are achieving for us an eternal glory that far outweighs them all. So we fix our eyes not on what is seen, but on what is unseen, since what is seen is temporary, but what is unseen is eternal."

Note 15: In Matthew 11:29, Jesus said, "Take my yoke upon you, and learn of me; for I am meek and lowly in heart: and ye shall find rest unto your souls." A few weeks ago, I thought I was going through some struggles. I made the mistake of looking at the outside, my circumstances, instead of looking inward to God for the answers. You see, it was all about my perspective. What I thought was a struggle was really a teachable moment. Through God's Word, He led me to my faults, to my correction and, direction and then to the lesson.

Something to think about: Maybe, just maybe, your struggle is not about your circumstances. Shift your perspective away from you and find out what God says about it in His Word. Maybe you will find out like I did, that the problem is really about how you respond to the struggle. Maybe your perceived struggle is actually a teachable moment where God is showing you that your response to the struggle is not aligned with His Word.

Note 16: Victory. Today I opened my Bible and landed on 1 Kings 19 that speaks, in part, on how the prophet Elijah fled for his life from Jezebel, the wife of King Ahab, and ended up under a juniper tree asking the Lord to take his life. The Lord had another plan for Elijah; and with the first visit, He touched Elijah and gave him food, water, and rest. But, on the Lord's second visit, the Lord touched Elijah again and told him to get up and eat in preparation for the journey.

Within my Bible study notes, there is a commentary: How often mountaintops of spiritual victory are followed by valleys and deserts of testing. Sometimes when life is going so great, when we feel blessed beyond measure, when we feel as if we are walking in victory and are on the edge of stepping into another level with God—those are the times when Satan will try his way with us. Your test might be a single lie sent to dilute your faith in what God has for you. Satan sent me such a thought. Not me, not now. My God has brought me, as the Old School people say, "A mighty long way." I didn't have a problem believing in and praising God during my struggles, and I certainly don't have a problem praising Him in victory. Satan get thee behind me, you are blocking my view of victory and I want everything that my God has for me!

Note 17: My struggles have not disappeared, but my mind and my heart have changed. Instead of complaining, the Holy Spirit directed me to look elsewhere—to myself, my mindset, my heart. Same struggles, different mind and heart, more peace.

Note 18: Happy. I have just been happy. I am still walking through my valley, but I am no longer focused on the journey, I am focused on what is at the end of the journey and I am excited with hope to discover what God has for me. This morning, I asked the Holy Spirit to guide my hand and I landed on 1 Samuel 30:18-19: "David recovered all that the Amalekites had taken, and David rescued his two wives. Nothing was missing, whether small or great, sons or daughters, spoil or anything that had been taken. David brought back all." Over the past several months, some peace has been taken from me. My journey has not changed, but I have. So, like David, God has restored what was taken from me—He has given me peace.

Following are several Bible Scriptures to help support and encourage you as God prepares you for your life's struggles and challenges. Believe me when I tell you, there is definitely a lesson in each, but there is also peace and joy on the other side. God is preparing you for something greater.

BIBLE SCRIPTURES

Psalm 37:1–5 ESV, Of David. Fret not yourself because of evildoers; be not envious of wrongdoers! For they will soon fade like the grass and wither like the green herb. Trust in the Lord, and do good; dwell in the land and befriend faithfulness. Delight yourself in the Lord, and He will give you the desires of your heart. Commit your way to the Lord; trust in Him, and He will act.

2 Corinthians 12:7–10 ESV, So to keep me from becoming conceited because of the surpassing greatness of the revelations, a thorn was given me in the flesh, a messenger of Satan to harass me, to keep me from becoming conceited. Three times I pleaded with the Lord about this, that it should leave me. But He said to me, "My grace is sufficient for you, for my power is made perfect in weakness." Therefore I will boast all the more gladly of my weaknesses, so that the power of Christ may rest upon me. For the sake of Christ, then, I am content with weaknesses, insults, hardships, persecutions, and calamities. For when I am weak, then I am strong.

Philippians 4:11–13 ESV, Not that I am speaking of being in need, for I have learned in whatever situation I am, to be content. I know how to be brought low, and I know how to abound. In any and every circumstance, I have learned the secret of facing plenty and hunger, abundance and need. I can do all things through Him who strengthens me.

1 Corinthians 10:13 ESV, No temptation has overtaken you that is not common to man. God is faithful, and He will not let you be tempted beyond your ability, but with the temptation, He will also provide the way of escape, that you may be able to endure it.

Jeremiah 1:19 ESV, They will fight against you, but they shall not prevail against you, for I am with you, declares the Lord, to deliver you."

Revelation 21:4 ESV, He will wipe away every tear from their eyes, and death shall be no more, neither shall there be mourning, nor crying, nor pain anymore, for the former things have passed away."

Psalm 34:17 ESV, When the righteous cry for help, the Lord hears and delivers them out of all their troubles.

Matthew 24:13 ESV, But the one who endures to the end will be saved.

APPLICATION

Often when we first wake up, we thank God and then as soon as our feet hit the floor, we start thinking about the struggles and challenges we will face throughout the day. I am reminded that God does not give us the spirit of fear and that He has everything I need. Even if our fear becomes our reality, He has got this. All I have to do is continue to meditate on His Word, be faithful, righteous and trust Him.

In Joshua, Chapter 1, God has commanded and directed Joshua to possess Jordan, the land God promised to His people, Israel. "Have I not commanded you? Be strong and courageous. Do not be afraid; do not be discouraged, for the Lord your God will be with you wherever you go" (Joshua 1:9). In Joshua 1:7-8, God tells Joshua to not waiver from the Word, to meditate on God's Word day and night, and then His way will be prosperous and have good success.

In order to get through our challenges and struggles, we need to see our circumstances for what they are: a test to authenticate who we say we are. Stop focusing on the struggle (the flesh) and focus on the lesson (acknowledging your weakness) and ask the Holy Spirit for revelation and direction. Know that your weakness gives your challenges and struggles power. If you say you are a Child of God and you are living a life of purpose, then you must act like it even in the midst of your troubles. Be quiet, stop complaining and blaming, pray, read and study the Word, then open your heart and mind to receive your correction, direction and revelation from the Holy Spirit.

As long as we live, we will have challenges and struggles. God is waiting on you to realize that you don't have the strength to fight your battles, but He does. Learn the lesson: Let go and accept that God is in control, not you

Below, briefly describe a challenge or struggle that you are going through or have recently gone through. Then, below it, in one word identify your weakness (pride, insecurity, control, stubbornness, procrastination, anger, jealousy, impenitence, etc.). And, finally, in one sentence, describe what you learned from the experience.

Describe your challenge or struggle:

_____

_____

_____

_____

Identify your weakness(es):

_____

_____

_____

_____

Identify the lesson learned:

_____

_____

_____

_____

Related topics: Chapter Two, Distractions and
Chapter Nine, Fear

CHAPTER NOTES

Here is your chance to write down a few thoughts of your own before we go to the next chapter.

_____

_____

_____

_____

_____

_____

_____

_____

_____

_____

_____

_____

_____

_____

_____

_____

_____

_____

_____

_____

_____

Chapter Fifteen

Bitterness

Connecting the dots: Bitterness seems justified at first, maybe even comforting. But in truth, bitterness is a destructive emotion that blinds your perspective while leading you along a path of self-righteousness.

Note 1: Be careful and guard your heart. Hate seems to be everywhere, distracting us from our true purpose.

Note 2: There is a connection between bitterness and iniquity. "But Peter said to him, 'Your money perish with you because you thought that the gift of God could be purchased with money! You have neither part nor portion in this matter, for your heart is not right in the sight of God. Repent therefore of this your wickedness, and pray God if perhaps the thought of your heart may be forgiven you. For I see that you are poisoned by bitterness and bound by iniquity'" (Acts 8: 20-23).

I am walking through a valley and I am not happy about it. My pride is causing bitterness to surface and I need to refresh my commitment to submit my cares to God. I am asking God to be faithful, so I must do the same with a righteous heart, and get back to where I belong. Next steps: I need to pray and confess my sins and ask for forgiveness and believe that God has everything under control. And, as I wait on Him and the victory that He promises—keep my thoughts, conversations, and actions in line with my faith knowing that God is in control, not me.

Note 3: I asked myself a question: If God told me that my bitterness was affecting my purpose (what God has created me to do), what would I do? My first thought was I would quickly get rid of the bitterness so that I could continue with what God has given me to do. Yesterday was a great day. I practiced what I teach and began the process of forgiving my enemies. Once I realized I was allowing bitterness to steal time and peace from me, the game changed. I am committed to having a righteous heart, to being happy, and walking in my purpose.

I know every day is not going to be easy. I will have random thoughts that need to be checked and redirected. But I can control my mouth. I know that words have power and I am flipping the game. So, not one word will I speak against my enemy. As was revealed to me: Don't focus on the flesh (the circumstances occurring), focus on the lesson. And the lesson is:

1. Stop focusing on the circumstances going on around me.

2. Be quiet and stop running my mouth and complaining.

3. Listen to the Holy Spirit and learn the lesson.

Following are several Bible Scriptures to help you see the damage bitterness causes in your life and in your spiritual growth.

BIBLE SCRIPTURES

Matthew 6:14–15 ESV, For if you forgive others their trespasses, your heavenly Father will also forgive you, but if you do not forgive others their trespasses, neither will your Father forgive your trespasses.

Hebrews 12:15 ESV, See to it that no one fails to obtain the grace of God; that no "root of bitterness" springs up and causes trouble, and by it many become defiled.

Ephesians 4:31–32 ESV, Let all bitterness and wrath and anger and clamor and slander be put away from you, along with all malice. Be kind to one another, tenderhearted, forgiving one another, as God in Christ forgave you.

Acts 8:23 ESV, For I see that you are in the gall of bitterness and in the bond of iniquity.

Ephesians 4:26 ESV, Be angry and do not sin; do not let the sun go down on your anger.

APPLICATION

Unchecked bitterness takes root, like dandelions in a field of grass. It might take a while to acknowledge that a spirit of bitterness has tucked itself away in your heart. Bitterness enjoys distracting your eagerness to be in God's presence; it chips away at your faith, clouds your purpose, and dilutes your praise.

How do you get back to God's presence? Ask for forgiveness, forgive your enemies, and ask God to forgive your enemies as well.

How do you forgive? As you have been forgiven—like Jesus did over and over again—with love, humility, obedience, and willingness and then, move on.

During my struggles, the Holy Spirit revealed that I must not focus on the flesh (people and circumstances), but instead focus on the lesson at hand. It is not my job to focus on the flesh or how I feel about my hurt, and disappointments. The Holy Spirit taught me that my job is to focus on the lesson unfolding in front of me and to maintain a righteous heart. Bitterness cannot take hold by itself. It needs our assistance to grow. The lesson within a struggle is to recognize your weakness and your sin, and to eventually forgive the people and/or the circumstances that hurt you.. If I choose not to forgive, then I am no better than my enemies and of no use to God.

Related topics: Chapter Two, Distractions; Chapter Nine, Fear; and Chapter Twenty, Forgiveness

CHAPTER NOTES

Here is your chance to write down a few thoughts of your own before we go to the next chapter.

_____

_____

_____

_____

_____

_____

_____

_____

_____

_____

_____

_____

_____

_____

_____

_____

_____

_____

_____

Chapter Sixteen

Prayer and Meditation

Connecting the dots: I have never won any battles by my own efforts. All of my battles have been won by prayer.

Note 1: Good morning, God! "And in the morning, rising up a great while before day, he went out and departed into a solitary place, and there prayed" (Mark 1:35). When I was a child, I used to see my father get up in the morning, kneel beside his bed, and pray. I was never close enough to hear his prayers, but I saw him praying. After all these years, that image of my father praying is still etched in my mind. And I have passed that gift on to my son, son Elijah so that he can know for himself the importance of communicating with God in the morning, throughout the day, and before he goes to sleep. Every day, when you wake up, open your eyes, and realize that God has already started a conversation with you. I mean, He didn't have to wake us up, but He did. So, it should not be difficult for us to continue the conversation and say, "Good morning, God. Thank you for blessing me with a new day and new opportunities to do your will."

Yes, you might still have the same problems you had the day before. But guess what? After praying and thanking God, your perspective should be more aligned with His. Yesterday has passed. Today is a brand-new day with new grace and new mercies. Good morning, God and thank you!

Note 2: You need to have a conversation with God. Tell Him what is bothering you. Tell Him what you are afraid of. Tell Him what you need. You cannot get over this obstacle until you surrender your problem and your life to God. He is waiting for you to offer this sacrifice. Nothing will be as it should until you offer God your problems and your life. You are wrestling with spiritual beings (Ephesians 6:12) that are determined to distract you from your purpose. But you must look beyond that and realize that Satan knows you have power and authority directly from Jesus Christ. If you continue to allow Satan to distract you, you will never realize the authority you have been given by God through Jesus Christ to change the circumstances in your life. So humble yourself and have a conversation with God; then listen for the Holy Spirit to give you revelation, correction, and direction.

Note 3: Pray and wait. In Luke 18:1-8, Jesus tells us that we should always pray and not lose heart, that we should be patient and persevere. We should not quit. God hears us when we pray, but He answers us in His own time, not ours. I am an impatient person; particularly when I know that my God is faithful and can do all things. In my mind (key point here, my mind), it seems reasonable to expect that my God will hear me and answer my prayer request quickly. And when I pray for relief from my enemies, or to right a wrong against me, I expect God to hurry and restore me. Here's the problem: in Luke 18:8, it says that God avenges speedily, which means quickly. God moves in His own time, not mine. I already know He is faithful, the real issue is will I be faithful and believe. He said I should trust Him, and I will. Pray for deliverance from evil people (Psalm 140). Pray for help in trouble (Psalm 141). Pray, be patient, and wait (Luke 18:1–8).

Note 4: What goes around, comes around. I think Psalm 141 is for the manipulating folks in our lives. Have you ever had the displeasure of being in the company of a manipulating person? Someone who constantly has some mess going on? Fake smile and fake laugh. Always talking bad about somebody (including you); throwing shade left and right. Always got a personal agenda to get ahead by stepping over someone else. Setting up people to fail, to wreck their marriages, their careers, to kill and destroy everything that is good. I try my best to stay away from manipulating people. They truly rub me the wrong way and my displeasure is transparent.

In Psalm 141, David starts a conversation with God and asks for help. In Psalm 141:1, David pleads with God to pay attention to him and to hear his cries. It seems there are people near David who work inequity (ill will) against him (and maybe others as well), setting snares and traps. David trusts God and, while he is in the middle of the mess and madness, he keeps his eyes on God. David asks God to restrain him—to keep his mouth closed and to not let him become evil and practice the same ill will. David also asks God to hem up the manipulators (workers of iniquity) in their own mess, so that they fall into their own traps.

As I learn more about prayer, I realize I need to talk with God when dealing with manipulating, people. It may seem like everything is working out for these people who work iniquity on others, but in the background, God has got everything under control and is working it out for good (Romans 8:28). Eventually, the people causing the ruckus in our lives will see and experience it for themselves.

Note 5: The Bible says that prayer changes things. "Then they cried to the Lord in their trouble, and He delivered them from their distress. He made the storm be still, and the waves of the sea were hushed. Then they were glad that the waters were quiet, and He brought them to their desired haven" (Psalm 107:28-30). I have been walking in my valley for more than a minute, and I am going to be honest. I am ready for this situation to change for the better. But there also needs to be a change in me. In order to get through this valley, I need more God in me and less Brinda. I need His presence, love, and protection, grace and mercy. I need guidance, knowledge, peace and wisdom. In my prayer, I need to have some honest conversations with God and tell Him how I feel and seek direction as He guides me through my valley.

Note 6: Meditation is when you think deeply or focus your mind for a period of time for religious or spiritual purposes, or as a method of relaxation. Oftentimes, we want people and situations to change. We cry out to God to do this and that for us. But what about a change in us? For example, learning to love ourselves, changing how we treat people, even how we reverence God and His Word. We can't change people or situations—but we can change through God's Word, which gives peace, knowledge, wisdom, healing and revelation. Here is the key: You have to believe it, meditate on it, and apply God's Word to your everyday life—consistently. When we read, we have a tendency to read over words without fully understanding the context or meaning. Take time and study God's Word with a Study Bible to get an understanding of what you are reading, and then apply that same understanding to your own life.

Note 7: In church, many of our pastors have a tradition of prompting us during service to say things like, "Now turn to your neighbor, take their hand tell them God is in control and everything is going to be alright". But what about us? Are we applying the same message of hope to our own lives? "I will meditate on your precepts (commandments) and fix my eyes on your ways. I will delight in your statutes (laws); I will not forget your word" (Psalm 119:15-16). The more you read and meditate on God's Word, and believe and apply God's Word to your life, the more change you will witness—not necessarily in other people or situations, but in you.

Following are several Bible Scriptures to help support the importance of prayer as a means to communicate and strengthen your relationship with God.

BIBLE SCRIPTURES

Mark 1:35 ESV, And rising very early in the morning, while it was still dark, He departed and went out to a desolate place, and there He prayed.

Proverbs 8:17 ESV, I love those who love me and those who seek me diligently find me.

Psalms 5:3 NKJV, My voice shalt thou hear in the morning, O LORD; in the morning will I direct [my prayer] unto thee, and will look up.

2 Chronicles 7:14 ESV, If my people who are called by my name humble themselves, and pray and seek my face and turn from their wicked ways, then I will hear from heaven and will forgive their sin and heal their land.

John 15:7 ESV, If you abide in me and my words abide in you, ask whatever you wish and it will be done for you.

Romans 8:26 ESV, Likewise the Spirit helps us in our weakness. For we do not know what to pray for as we ought, but the Spirit himself intercedes for us with groanings too deep for words.

Matthew 26:41 ESV, Watch and pray that you may not enter into temptation. The spirit indeed is willing, but the flesh is weak.

James 5:16 ESV, Therefore, confess your sins to one another and pray for one another, that you may be healed. The prayer of a righteous person has great power as it is working.

Psalm 1:1–3 ESV, Blessed is the man who walks not in the counsel of the wicked, nor stands in the way of sinners, nor sits in the seat of scoffers; but his delight is in the law of the Lord, and on his law he meditates day and night. He is like a tree planted by streams of water that yields its fruit in its season, and its leaf does not wither. In all that he does, he prospers.

Isaiah 26:3 ESV, You keep him in perfect peace whose mind is stayed on you, because he trusts in you.

Psalm 19:14 ESV, Let the words of my mouth and the meditation of my heart be acceptable in your sight, O Lord, my rock and my redeemer.

APPLICATION

Prayer is simply a vertical conversation with God. I am discovering that prayer is less about me telling God about my problems, what I want, or how I feel. He knows all that stuff anyway. Prayer is more about me coming to God, worshiping and praising Him, and hearing what He has to say.

In Psalm 140, David prays to God for deliverance from his enemies. We all can relate to David and his need for deliverance. Psalm 140 reminds us that we need to tell God about our problems, about people that plan evil, and speak against us. It reminds us that we can ask God for help to take us out of any evil situation and cover and protect us from traps set by our enemies. Eventually, those same enemies will be hunted and overthrown by the very evil they planned for us. We should be confident in knowing that God is faithful and will maintain us in every situation. At the end of Psalm 140, after David speaks with God and unburdens himself, it seems David remembers that if he is righteous and seeks God's covering and strength that he can reside in God's presence. And for this, David was thankful to God.

We need to make time for prayer with God, and tell Him what is going on with us as we seek His covering and strength. In God's presence, talking with Him, that is where we will find peace from our struggles. I challenge to you to start and end every day with prayer.

Related topics: Chapter Eleven, Our Relationship With God and Chapter Nineteen, Praise

CHAPTER NOTES

Here is your chance to write down a few thoughts of your own before we go to the next chapter.

_____

_____

_____

_____

_____

_____

_____

_____

_____

_____

_____

_____

_____

_____

_____

_____

_____

_____

_____

_____

_____

Chapter Seventeen

Meekness

Connecting the dots: Jesus's journey from the Garden of Gethsemane to dying on the cross is my model of meekness.

Note 1: My studies on overcoming struggles led me to study sin of pride which is so subtle that we don't realize how interwoven it is within our struggles. Studying pride, led me to study the virtue of meekness. Driving to work one day, I thought, what exactly does meekness look like? How am I to respond when people come against me, when I feel betrayed, when I am confronted or in the midst of a struggle? I thought the ultimate image and application of meekness could only be found in God's Word. So, I read and studied Matthew 26, which provides us with the beautiful lesson of Jesus, our Lord and Savior humbling Himself as He prepares to die on the cross for our sins.

Note 2: Jesus is my example of meekness (Matthew 26). We easily run to and grasp the parts of God's Word that tell us we are, for example, "wonderfully and fearfully made"; that we are a Child of God; that we are blessed, victorious, etc. But it is difficult to take on and cover myself in God's Word without applying it to my everyday life. I cannot be an example to myself and others seeking to know God, if I don't know how to act; that is, to acknowledge my pride and learn to follow Jesus' example of being meek, yet being strong through Him.

I have learned that meekness has nothing to do with being weak. It is about being strong. How is that? When we feel we have been wronged, it takes a lot to not complain, or be bitter, resentful, jealous, etc. It takes patience, perseverance, and actively adjusting our attitude back from the situation at hand and focusing on God's will, which we know and believe will ultimately work in our favor. As I said, it takes a lot, but all we can do is pray for God to strengthen us as we wait and keep our hearts, thoughts, attitude, and mouths (yes, because we often talk too much and complain and spread strife when we are hurting) focused on the future victory. It is hard, but as I learn more about pride and meekness, I have been more at peace. The situations and struggles have not changed, but I have for the better.

Note 3: Meekness is one of the nine virtues that should be demonstrated in a Child of God. We often confuse the meanings of the words *meekness* and *humble*. The word *humble* is based on action. *Meekness* deals with our mind and hearts—internal attitudes. It is difficult to be patient and maintain the right internal attitude and be like Jesus Christ (our model and teacher). I am definitely still learning and practicing being meek. Our efforts at practicing meekness should be measured against Christ's meekness—His humility, patience, and total submission of His own will to the will of the Father.

Note 4: While continuing my reading of Matthew 26, today's revelation is that it's not always about what I perceive is happening, but instead about the reality of how I respond to what I believe is happening. If we respond with pride, bitterness, and anger, resentment will follow. But if we are mindful to submit ourselves to God's will, our response (heart and attitude) of meekness (as demonstrated by Jesus Christ and not as defined by *Webster's Dictionary*) will bring us less stress, less strife, and more time to focus on persevering to the victory that God has promised to us.

Note 5: When I am going through a personal journey, I have a tendency to complain along the way. Why? Because I am selfish and spoiled and I'd rather be comfortable and showered with blessings instead of strife. This morning, as I did a quick Bible study on complaining, I had an eye opening experience when I turned to Philippians 2:1-18, in which the Apostle Paul teaches on the mindset or attitude of harmonious thinking. Particularly in Philippians 2:14-15, Christians are not to complain so that we can be an example in the middle of a crooked and perverse generation. My complaining comes from unfulfilled desires (what I want), which leads to internal and external strife along my journey. Rather than complain, I am supposed to use Christ as my example, assume a servant's position and humble myself. Ouch!

Next are several Bible scriptures to help support the application of meekness modeled by our Lord and Savior, Jesus into our daily lives.

BIBLE SCRIPTURES

Isaiah 53:7 ESV, He was oppressed, and he was afflicted, yet he opened not his mouth; like a lamb that is led to the slaughter, and like a sheep that before its shearers is silent, so he opened not his mouth.

Matthew 11:29 ESV, Take my yoke upon you, and learn from me, for I am gentle and lowly in heart, and you will find rest for your souls.

Psalm 25:9 ESV, He leads the humble in what is right, and teaches the humble His way.

Matthew 5:5 ESV, Blessed are the meek, for they shall inherit the earth.

Philippians 2:14–16 ESV, Do all things without grumbling or questioning, that you may be blameless and innocent, children of God without blemish in the midst of a crooked and twisted generation, among whom you shine as lights in the world, holding fast to the word of life, so that in the day of Christ I may be proud that I did not run in vain or labor in vain.

1 Peter 3:4 ESV, But let your adorning be the hidden person of the heart with the imperishable beauty of a gentle and quiet spirit, which in God's sight is very precious.

Psalm 37:11 ESV, But the meek shall inherit the land and delight themselves in abundant peace.

APPLICATION

I now know that some of my challenges and struggles were the result of my pride and that I need to focus on being more like Jesus, who said in Matthew 11:29, "I am meek and lowly in heart." Had I had a mindset of being "meek and lowly in heart," I would have avoided quite a few challenges and struggles.

So now I ask, in what areas of your own life should you apply Jesus Christ, as your model of meekness? Please list at least three areas below, and follow my example: *I should listen to other people when they are talking, rather than interrupt them.*

1. _____

2. _____

3. _____

Related topics: Chapter Five, Renew Me and
Chapter Eighteen, Faithfulness

CHAPTER NOTES

Here is your chance to write down a few thoughts of your own before we go to the next chapter.

_____

_____

_____

_____

_____

_____

_____

_____

_____

_____

_____

_____

_____

_____

_____

_____

_____

_____

_____

Chapter Eighteen

Faithfulness

❦ ❦

Connecting the dots: He said, "Trust me"–and I will.

Note 1: For nearly every situation we go through, and just maybe all situations, Romans 8:28 continually rings true: And we (*you and me*) know (*have faith in, believe*) that for those who love God (*acknowledge Him, love Him, praise and worship Him, submit to Him, obey Him, do His will*) all things (*life, death, disasters, miracles, our jobs, our marriages and relationships, our children, our health, our finances, the world, the universe, the weather, even politics*), work together for good (*are designed to work out according to God's plan, not ours*), for those (*you and me*) who are called (*Believers*) according to His purpose (*God's will, not our own*). Basically, God is in control. Everything and everybody will work out as He has planned.

Note 2: "But blessed is the one who trusts in the Lord, whose confidence is in him. They will be like a tree planted by the water that sends out its roots by the stream. It does not fear when heat comes; its leaves are always green. It has no worries in a year of drought and never fails to bear fruit". (Jeremiah 17:7–8). I am blessed when I trust in the Lord and put my confidence in Him. I will be like a tree planted by the water that sends out its roots by the stream. I will not fear when heat comes; my leaves will always be green. I will have no worries in a year of drought and I will never fail to produce fruit.

Note 3: Even when everything is changing and I may not agree; when enemies come against me; when my pride gets the best of me—my God said, "Trust me." So, I will; so I must. "Trust in the Lord with all your heart, and do not lean on your own understanding. In all your ways acknowledge Him, and He will make straight your paths. Be not wise in your own eyes; fear the Lord, and turn away from evil. It will be healing to your flesh and refreshment to your bones" (Proverbs 3:5–8).

Note 4: Yesterday, I was disappointed over something I wanted badly. I prayed in faith and believed God would bless me with this desire. But I didn't get what I wanted. When I heard the news, I was taken back a bit because I believed, walking in faith, that it was already a reality. I didn't get what I wanted, but I did notice that I took the news in stride, which was a surprise to me. I even told my husband I was ok with it. Why? Because God has never failed me. He has always given me way more than I deserve and I know that He has something better for me.

The next morning when I woke up, the first thing on my mind was the disappointment. But I turned my thoughts to God's Word and thanked Him for what He has already done. God's Word says in Romans 8:28 (KJV): "And we know that all things work together for good to them that love God, to them who are the called according to His purpose." And Proverbs 3:5-6 says: "Trust in the Lord with all your heart, and do not lean on your own understanding. In all your ways acknowledge Him, and He will make straight your paths."

Yes, I was a bit disappointed, but I knew God had it all under control and I just need to go along for the ride and trust Him. Maybe God said no to keep me from something or someone, or to keep me from harm or danger. Maybe it would have distracted me from my purpose. I don't know. Only God knows His reasons and I have to be fine with that. He said trust Him, and I do.

Following are several Bible Scriptures to help support faithfulness. Faith has two sides, what God will do and what you are supposed to do.

BIBLE SCRIPTURES

Deuteronomy 7:9 ESV, Know therefore that the Lord your God is God, the faithful God who keeps covenant and steadfast love with those who love Him and keep His commandments to a thousand generations.

Lamentations 3:22–23 ESV, The steadfast love of the Lord never ceases; His mercies never come to an end; they are new every morning; great is your faithfulness.

2 Thessalonians 3:3 ESV, But the Lord is faithful. He will establish you and guard you against the evil one.

Hebrews 10:23 ESV, Let us hold fast the confession of our hope without wavering, for He who promised is faithful.

Hebrews 12:1–2 ESV, Therefore, since we are surrounded by so great a cloud of witnesses, let us also lay aside every weight, and sin which clings so closely, and let us run with endurance the race that is set before us, looking to Jesus, the founder and perfecter of our faith, who for the joy that was set before him endured the cross, despising the shame, and is seated at the right hand of the throne of God.

Hebrews 11:6 ESV, And without faith it is impossible to please Him, for whoever would draw near to God must believe that He exists and that He rewards those who seek Him.

Philippians 3:12–14 ESV, Not that I have already obtained this or am already perfect, but I press on to make it my own because Christ Jesus has made me His own. Brothers, I do not consider that I have made it my own. But one thing I do: forgetting what lies behind and straining forward to what lies ahead, I press on toward the goal for the prize of the upward

APPLICATION

God gives us His Word but it is up to us to receive it, believe it, and act on it. Our responsiveness and application to His Word opens up new opportunities to exercise our faith.

In September 2018, God tested me on faith; and initially, I did not do so well on my test. Reading Hebrews 11, I started to see a deeper perspective of faith—not just what God can do—but what I am supposed to do with no fear, questions, or wavering. Not easy for a controlling person—hence the reason for the test. After reading Hebrews 11, I was ashamed of my lack of faith and short sightedness.

One of the greatest days of my life was when my teenage son, Elijah, spoke the Word to me. He lightened my heart and basically told me to press on and do what God has told me to do and that it will be a platform to help other people. I thank God for my son and husband, Eddie, who have shown me their faith while I questioned this test.

Google The Message Bible version and read Hebrews 11. Then, in no more than three sentences, describe below a significant test that God gave you over the past year which took you out of your comfort zone. After you finish, write one sentence of how God showed you He was faithful.

_____

_____

_____

_____

_____

Related topics: Chapter Ten, Focus and Chapter Eleven, Our Relationship with God

CHAPTER NOTES

Here is your chance to write down a few thoughts of your own before we go to the next chapter.

_____

_____

_____

_____

_____

_____

_____

_____

_____

_____

_____

_____

_____

_____

_____

_____

_____

_____

Chapter Nineteen

Praise

⚜ ⚜

Connecting the dots: Our praise is a reflection of our character.

Note 1: This week I considered the question, what is the quality of my praise.? As we learn about and truly accept God's love for us, we begin to realize how valuable we are and we want to reciprocate the love we have received. Just like lovers, we desire to please God. As our relationship with Him grows and our life is renewed, we desire to speak and think in ways favorable to Him. Eventually, our purpose-driven lifestyle should be a reflection of God's Glory.

God's love for me creates my value and my gratitude for His patience, grace, and mercy over my life impacts my praise. We use our mouths to praise God and we praise Him with thanksgiving, an upright heart, and willfully. We were all created by God for a purpose so there are no accidents in His plans. However, if we are burdened with personal issues and distractions, we will be challenged to praise God with a thankful and upright heart in pursuit of purpose.

I believe the biggest obstacle in our lives is that we let personal issues take hold of us for years. Our issues impact how we think, live, speak, love, respond, and praise God. How? The same mouth that we use to praise God, we with hearts of unrighteousness, use to speak words of fear, insecurity, pride, jealousy, lust, envy, blasphemy, hate, gossip, anger, and selfishness. The quality of my praise is better because I am more focused on my words and my intent. I can never be perfect, but I can be better.

Note 2: In Isaiah 43:21 (NKJV), God speaks: "This people I have formed for Myself; They shall declare My praise." I had never taken the time to really think about the act of praising God, but as I study about praise, I realize that it is much more than simply lifting my hands. The Bible verse above presents a command in the words "They shall." Because I am a Child of God, I understand and agree that I will praise my God. But because I want to give my God the best I have, I asked myself, "Brinda, what is the quality of your praise?" Because I had no answer to the question, there must be room for improvement.

Note 3: Not long ago, I drove past the first house I purchased when I was twenty-seven A few weeks later, I drove past the second house I owned when I was in my early thirties. I thought about the old Brinda that lived in those houses. Looking back on how damaged I was emotionally and spiritually—Oh, my God! I have to thank Him! He didn't have to change me, but He did. He didn't have to wait for me, but He did. He didn't have to love me, forgive me, heal me, bless me, shower me with undeserved grace, nor favor me over and over again—but He did. Think back on your own life and all that God has done for you and brought you through. Truly our God is worthy to be praised!

Note 4: "Whoever guards his mouth preserves his life; he who opens wide his lips comes to ruin" (Proverbs 13:3). When I think about the quality of my praise, the first thing that comes to mind is we talk too much about nothing. We spend too much time talking about things that do not matter. Over the past year, it seems there has been no shortage of news and defiling topics for us to absorb and discuss. Yes, we live in a world with others and we can never fully get away, but we can pay more attention and do better and speak words of life instead of death. Positive words instead of negative. Kind words instead of cruel words. Encouraging words instead of jealous ones. Less mess and more praise.

Following are several Bible Scriptures to help support the importance of praising God in our lives..

BIBLE SCRIPTURES

1 Chronicles 16:29 ESV, Ascribe to the Lord the glory due to His name; bring an offering and come before Him! Worship the Lord in the splendor of holiness.

Hebrews 13:15 ESV, Through Him then let us continually offer up a sacrifice of praise to God, that is, the fruit of lips that acknowledge His name.

Psalm 117:1-2 ESV, Praise the Lord, all nations! Extol Him, all peoples! For great is His steadfast love toward us, and the faithfulness of the Lord endures forever. Praise the Lord!

Psalm 146:1–2 ESV, Praise the Lord! Praise the Lord, O my soul! I will praise the Lord as long as I live; I will sing praises to my God while I have my being.

APPLICATION

We praise God because He created us and everything else. Therefore, He alone is worthy of our praise. Our condition when we praise should be:

• with thanksgiving.

• with an upright heart.

• willfully. Our praise is free and not forced.

We can praise God:

• with our mouths.

• as we sing.

• in our songs.

Now that I have some information on praise, I can see that there is truly room for improvement in the praise that I give God.

Related topics: Chapter Twelve, Words Have Power and Chapter Twenty-One, Gratitude

CHAPTER NOTES

Here is your chance to write down a few thoughts of your own before we go to the next chapter.

Chapter Twenty

Forgiveness

Connecting the dots: Forgiveness is the hardest thing for us to do, but it is also the easiest for us to receive.

Note 1: Lord, please forgive me for thinking too small. This week, I failed yet another test. A person at work keeps confronting me; even when time after time, I do my best to be positive, to walk in faith, and to speak well to him. This week, he and I just didn't agree. My spirit is uneasy around him and I do not trust him. I cannot understand why he keeps coming after me like someone seeking revenge.

But as I stand in church service, worshiping you, I realize that I have been walking in pride and fear. I feared this person's words and deeds against me and believed that he could take what I have built. I realize he can take what I created, but he cannot take what You have given me.

Over the past two years, you, Lord, have answered all my prayers. You have moved evil people out of my path and placed good people there instead. You have taken my problems and weaved them into opportunities. In my pride, I thought I was creating something. So, when I thought this person was trying to take what was mine, I became angry and weak and allowed my flesh and thoughts to condemn me. Now, I realize I have sinned. Forgive me, Father, for thinking small, for forgetting that you are God and I am not, for walking in fear. Forgive me, Lord, for forgetting that what You created for me is much greater than anything that my mind and hands could ever conceive and that what You create and give me, no one can ever take from me. No one can take away the talents and gifts You have given me to use, the blessings that refresh and encourage me. So again, I am sorry, Lord, for thinking too small. Please, forgive me. I cannot ever think and live small when I am a Child of God.

Note 2: Yesterday was an emotional day, but I stood on my square and the importance of my purpose was confirmed again— not softly, but loud and clear. I had a frank conversation with a family member that has decades of residual personal issues. Residual because they never took the time to look at their issues, instead always looking at how someone else did them wrong. If you feel someone hurt you (real or perceived), forgive them and then ask God to forgive you. Don't spend decades walking around with old issues (real or perceived), hurting yourself and others because you feel somebody owes you something. God already gave you everything you need and has promised you much more; but first, you need to forgive that person and then ask God to forgive you. You can continue to be stubborn about it if you want, or even take it to your grave, but tell me, how is that stubbornness working out for you so far?

Following are several Bible Scriptures to help support our need to forgive.

BIBLE SCRIPTURES

Colossians 3:13 ESV, Bearing with one another and if one has a complaint against another, forgiving each other; as the Lord has forgiven you, so you also must forgive.

Luke 6:37 ESV, Judge not, and you will not be judged; condemn not, and you will not be condemned; forgive, and you will be forgiven.

Mark 11:25 ESV, And whenever you stand praying, forgive, if you have anything against anyone, so that your Father also who is in heaven may forgive you your trespasses.

Ephesians 4:32 ESV, Be kind to one another, tenderhearted, forgiving one another, as God in Christ forgave you.

Proverbs 10:12 ESV, Hatred stirs up strife, but love covers all offenses.

Proverbs 19:11 ESV, Good sense makes one slow to anger, and it is His glory to overlook an offense.

APPLICATION

Forgiveness is the key to protecting your purpose. Our struggles reveal our weaknesses and should be catalysts for our spiritual growth. We grow spiritually by letting go of the past with forgiveness and reaching forward to embrace what God has for us. It is hard to reach for what God has when your heart is full of hurt and bitterness from the past. Forgiveness is key to your happiness and protecting your purpose.

How does this work? Three words:

Humble

Obedient

Willingness

Jesus is not only our Lord and Savior, He is our Teacher and our model as we live our lives of purpose. Read and study Jesus' walk to the cross as illustrated in Matthew, Luke, and John and see forgiveness another way—the gift that Jesus gave to us, which we are to give to others.

Below, list three people you need to forgive and let go of. Think about how your negative feelings and thoughts have kept you bound emotionally. Try looking at each person as human, flawed, and in need of understanding and forgiveness—just like you. It's hard, I know, but it's a start to forgiveness and a happier life.

1._____

2._____

3._____

Related topics: Chapter Seven, The Power of Purpose and Chapter Nine, Fear

CHAPTER NOTES

Here is your chance to write down a few thoughts of your own
before we go to the next chapter.

_____

_____

_____

_____

_____

_____

_____

_____

_____

_____

_____

_____

_____

_____

_____

_____

_____

_____

Chapter Twenty-One

Gratitude

Connecting the dots: Thank you, God, for all you have done for me. You are faithful in every situation, even when I am not.

Note 1: God speaks to us in many ways: through His Word; His Son, Jesus Christ; prayer; our circumstances; in others; nature; and in music. I also believe God speaks to us as He allows us to breathe and gives us yet another opportunity to reflect His Glory in our everyday lives. This morning, think about God's sovereignty, love, goodness, mercy, favor, provision, protection, and friendship; then, open your mouth and say, "Good morning, God. Thank you for this day."

Note 2: My gratitude increased significantly when I challenged my attitude and realized that it's not about me. It's all about God and His plans and purpose for my life.

Note 3: I am grateful for my life and the countless ways God has blessed me. Before God changed my life, I was not always grateful and did not appreciate Him or His blessings. But I now realize, I was never worthy yet He blessed me anyway. Gratitude was the starting point of my salvation. Thank you, God, for another day.

Note 4: I am not on your time. I am not on my time. I am on God's time. Every moment I waste on arguing and being mad is wasting His time. Every moment I spend forgetting that I have been healed by His stripes, that I can do all things, that I am beauty made in His image, that I am His child, that He died so that I might live, are moments when I waste time. I am not here for me; I am here to proclaim the Gospel and to do God's will. Period.

Following are several Bible Scriptures to help support our need to feel and express gratitude for all that God has done for use.

BIBLE SCRIPTURES

John 3:16 ESV, "For God so loved the world, that He gave His only Son, that whoever believes in Him should not perish but have eternal life.

Psalm 9:1 ESV, I will give thanks to the Lord with my whole heart; I will recount all of your wonderful deeds.

James 1:17 ESV, Every good gift and every perfect gift is from above, coming down from the Father of lights, with whom there is no variation or shadow due to change.

1 Thessalonians 5:16–18 ESV, Rejoice always, pray without ceasing, give thanks in all circumstances; for this is the will of God in Christ Jesus for you.

Psalm 28:7 ESV, The Lord is my strength and my shield; in Him my heart trusts, and I am helped; my heart exults, and with my song, I give thanks to Him.

Colossians 3:15–17 ESV, And let the peace of Christ rule in your hearts, to which indeed you were called in one body. And be thankful. Let the word of Christ dwell in you richly, teaching and admonishing one another in all wisdom, singing psalms and hymns and spiritual songs, with thankfulness in your hearts to God. And whatever you do, in word or deed, do everything in the name of the Lord Jesus, giving thanks to God the Father through Him.

APPLICATION

Today, thank God for another today which is like none other. Thank you, Lord, for another opportunity to do your will. Today, more of you, Lord, and less of me.

Related topics: Chapter Eleven, Our Relationship With God and Chapter Nineteen, Praise

CHAPTER NOTES

Here is your chance to write down a few thoughts of your own before we go to the next chapter.

_____

_____

_____

_____

_____

_____

_____

_____

_____

_____

_____

_____

_____

_____

_____

_____

_____

_____

Chapter Twenty-Two

Peace

Connecting the dots: Peace, like happiness, requires work.

Note 1: If you had to separate all people into just two person-ality types, I would be in the Type A column. Type A and Type B personality theory describes two contrasting personality types. In this theory, personalities that are more competitive, outgo-ing, ambitious, impatient, and/or aggressive are labeled Type A; while more relaxed personalities are labeled Type B. As a Type A personality, my personal journey has been more difficult. Last week, as I learned more about prayer and applied it to my own life, God gave me peace, and I love it and I want to enjoy it for as long as I can.

My advice to myself and fellow Type A personalities: once you feel better, don't run toward any mess. Slow down, take some time, and relax. Enjoy every moment of your peace. Through-out your days, thank God for the peace He has given you, peace that surpasses all understanding. Live in the moment. Bask and refresh yourself in the peace that God has given you. and, when you feel yourself slipping (you know eventually you will because you are a Type A), remember what you have learned and talk to

God in prayer and let Him handle it all. "And the peace of God, which surpasses all understanding, will guard your hearts and your minds in Christ Jesus" (Philippians 4:7).

Note 2: Yesterday God led me to Jeremiah 17 and restored my peace. Then to 1 John 3:19-24 and comforted me. You can't tell me there is no God. To simply read words on paper that speak specifically to my spirit and touch what is wrong and replace it with joy and peace—is proof to me of God's existence. Thank you, Lord.

You need to have a strong mind and continually seek the presence of God in order to walk through your life distractions, fears (e.g., pride, insecurity, procrastination, self-condemnation, and denial), regrets, changes, and setbacks. Recognize that Satan comes to steal your joy, your peace, your love, your faith, and your purpose. Stay focused on God's Word and all the lessons you have learned in your journey as a Child of God and hold your ground and be certain to wear your armor of God every day— faith, righteousness, God's Word, peace, salvation, and truth. I refuse to go backward; I am determined to only go forward.

Following are several Bible Scriptures to help support the peace God gives us as we align ourselves to His will.

BIBLE SCRIPTURES

Isaiah 26:3 ESV, You keep him in perfect peace whose mind is stayed on you, because he trusts in you.

1 Peter 5:6–7 ESV, Humble yourselves, therefore, under the mighty hand of God so that at the proper time He may exalt you, casting all your anxieties on Him because He cares for you.

Philippians 4:6 ESV, Do not be anxious about anything, but in everything by prayer and supplication with thanksgiving, let your requests be made known to God.

1 Peter 3:9–11 ESV, Do not repay evil for evil or reviling for reviling, but on the contrary, bless, for to this you were called, that you may obtain a blessing. For "Whoever desires to love life and see good days, let him keep his tongue from evil and his lips from speaking deceit; let him turn away from evil and do good; let him seek peace and pursue it.

APPLICATION

Have you ever had a problem or situation just weigh on you? Have you ever thought you had the strength to carry on, but found out that you could not? Have you ever found yourself pressed up against a wall, emotions spent, with no options left? I am going to guess that your answer is yes. Do you know we can prolong our stress and anxiety by holding on to our cares instead of taking them to God? The answer is, Yes!We can get relief from our problems and situations by taking them to God in prayer. And at the end of that conversation, there is peace.

In the Bible, we are told to pray in the morning and at night, to pray constantly, to pray in troubles, to pray when our enemies come against us, and when we are afraid. We are also told to pray for those in authority over us, which can be hard to do when we perceive they are the source of our stress and discontent. In Psalm 55:22, we are told to "Cast your cares on the LORD and He will sustain you; He will never let the righteous be shaken" and in 1 Peter 5:7, we are told to "Give all your worries and cares to God, for He cares about you."

If you are going through something big or small, begin the practice of taking your concerns to God in prayer. Have your conversation with God and take the time to hear Him. Your problems may still surround you, but in the midst of being in God's presence, He will give you peace.

Related topics: Chapter Six, Purpose and Chapter Sixteen, Prayer and Meditation

CHAPTER NOTES

Here is your chance to write down a few thoughts of your own before we go to the next chapter.

_____

_____

_____

_____

_____

_____

_____

_____

_____

_____

_____

_____

_____

_____

_____

_____

_____

_____

Conclusion

I am hopeful that reading this book will help you connect the dots of your journey as you apply God's Word in your life and discover the importance of living a life of purpose.

Living a life of purpose is not easy, but it is wonderful and fulfilling, in ways you never imagined. As you grow spiritually by reading, studying, and applying God's Word in your life, you might find that life seems more difficult and that there are more obstacles at home, at your job, with your friends, and conflicts within yourself. Don't be surprised when this happens. There will be days of uncertainty and fear; even days of great sadness and weakness—but you will get through them. In these moments, God is doing a great work in you. He is pulling off the old and making room for the new you (Psalm 18:19).

Submit yourself and allow God to make you into the authentic creation He designed and planned ages ago; before the world took hold of you and hurt you. God will pull away every hurt, but you must submit yourself and allow Him to do the healing. All these years you have been in mourning for what you lost; God has come to restore you back to Him and His plans, not yours.

Realize, your authentication process never ends. You will not be made perfect until our Lord Jesus returns to rule. Each day you are being authenticated and tested, prove to be who you confess that you are, a Believer, a Child of God, living a life of purpose.

Every day provides new opportunities for us to grow spiritually. God does not test us to hurt us, but to help us acknowledge and learn from our weakness.

In my authentication process, I came to realize that my weaknesses of pride, insecurity, and fear were triggers that I used to amplify and make my challenges and struggles more difficult. Once I started paying less attention to the challenge or struggle (the test) and more attention to the lesson, I realized that my job was to not respond with pride, insecurity, or fear but to submit and learn the lesson which is this: God is in control. When I submit my challenges and struggles to God, He will take care of them, in His way and in His time. While I wait on God to work it out for my good, I stay faithful, stay righteous, and ask the Holy Spirit to reveal my weakness and tell me what to do. Then, being obedient to the Holy Spirit, I study God's Word and apply it in my life with Jesus Christ as my model and teacher.

Our goal should be to learn the lessons within each challenge or struggle and try our best to not repeat them. However, we are human and there will be many days when you miss the mark. Don't worry. You will keep repeating the same struggle presented in different ways over and over until you learn the lesson. Eventually, you will get better at recognizing when your weakness has been triggered and you will apply the lesson learned and move on.

With each victory, we learn to trust God more and we begin to see ourselves more as God sees us, we begin to see the Child God created us to be, full of love, power, talents, and gifts—all to live a life of purpose and to do His will.

Right now, in my journey, I feel lighter and free. Letting go of my past and practicing forgiveness has opened my mind and heart to new ideas and I no longer feel bound by my weaknesses or past hurts.

I pray that you have enjoyed this book and that what I have shared from my journey will bless you in yours. If you have not already done so, I encourage you to find a Christian, Word-driven, teaching church and find a means to keep accountable to this life of purpose. Take Bible study classes, read the Bible for yourself, study on your own, keep a journal (written or electronic) of your journey, encircle yourself with like-minded and life-minded people. And, most importantly, pray and stay in God's presence every day. Ask the Holy Spirit for revelation and instruction, and listen for the lessons that unfold. Then, be obedient and do what you are told, which often involves correction and forgiveness. As you go through your own authentication process, get out of the way and put Jesus Christ, our Lord, in front of every situation and follow Him.

He told me to trust Him, and I do.

With Love,

Brinda Devine

P.S. Because the *authentication process* never ends, I will continue to share my spiritual growth on the following platforms:

www.brindadevine.com

www.purpose8institute.com

www.facebook.com/discoveryourpurpose8

Instagram @brindadevine

Appendix

Spiritual Gifts

Spiritual gifts are given by God to every human and are controlled by the Holy Spirit. Spiritual gifts are not human talents and abilities. Some Believers operate in their spiritual gifts daily, some periodically, and others only for an appointed time. And, some people are called by God to minister and hold office in their spiritual gifts.

SPIRITUAL GIFTS HAVE THREE PURPOSES:

1) to equip the Body of Christ (that is, the Church made up of all those that have accepted Jesus Christ as their personal Savior) for the work of the ministry (discovery and activation of their spiritual gifts);

2) for building up (edifying and maturing) the body of Christ;

3) and to glorify God.

To gain a better understanding of spiritual gifts, first read a Study Bible. Then, to support your learning, read books and articles on the topic of spiritual gifts. There are many Study Bibles to choose from, that can be purchased or found online. I use *The King James Study Bible* by Thomas Nelson Publishers and *The Ministry Gifts* by Kenneth E. Hagin.

For the most part, spiritual gifts are discussed in these Bible Scriptures:

Romans 12:4–8 ESV, For as in one body we have many members, and the members do not all have the same function, so we, though many, are one body in Christ, and individually, members one of another. Having gifts that differ according to the grace given to us, let us use them: if **prophecy,** in proportion to our faith; if service, in our **serving;** the one who teaches, in His **teaching;** the one who **exhorts,** in His exhortation; the one who **contributes,** in generosity; the one who **leads,** with zeal; the one who does **acts of mercy,** with cheerfulness.

1 Corinthians 12:8–10 ESV For to one is given through the Spirit the utterance of **wisdom,** and to another the utterance of **knowledge** according to the same Spirit, to another **faith** by the same Spirit, to another gifts of **healing** by the one Spirit, to another the **working of miracles,** to another **prophecy,** to another the ability **to distinguish between spirits,** to another **various kinds of tongues,** to another **the interpretation of tongues.**

1 Corinthians 12:27–28 ESV Now you are the body of Christ and individually members of it. And God has appointed in the church first **apostles,** second **prophets,** third **teachers,** then **miracles,** then gifts of **healing, helping, administrating,** and **various kinds of tongues.**

Ephesians 4:11–12 ESV And He gave **the apostles, the prophets, the evangelists, the shepherds and teachers,** to equip the saints for the work of the ministry, for building up the body of Christ, one **who exhorts,** in His exhortation; the one **who contributes,** in generosity; the one **who leads,** with zeal; the one who **does acts of mercy,** with cheerfulness.

Spiritual Gifts in Scripture			
Romans 12–48	**1 Corinthians 12:8–10**	**1 Corinthians 12:27–28**	**Ephesians 4:11–12**
Prophecy	Word of Wisdom	Apostles	Apostles
Serving	Word of Knowledge	Prophets	Prophets
Teaching	Faith	Teachers	Evangelists
Exhortation	Healing	Miracles	Shepherds
Contributor (Giver)	Working of Miracles	Healing	Teachers
Leader	Prophecy	Helping	Exhorter
Mercy (Kindness)	Distinguish between spirits (Discerning of Spirits)	Administration (Guiding)	Contributor (Giver)
	Various Kinds of Tongues	Various Kinds of Tongues	Leader
	Interpretation of Tongues		Mercy (Kindness)

Categories of Spiritual Gifts		
Gifts of Revelation	Gifts of Demonstration	Gifts of Inspiration
Word of Knowledge	Gift of Faith	Gift of Prophecy
Word of Wisdom	Working of Miracles	Gift of Tongues
Discerning of spirits	Gifts of Healing	Interpretation of Tongues

Glossary

Below are definitions I have compiled after reading and studying a variety of sources about spiritual gifts. For your own understanding of each spiritual gift, I suggest you read and study the Bible, confirm what you already know about yourself, and open your heart and spirit to a new revelation of God's plans for you.

Administration: Those with this spiritual gift guide the body of Christ toward accomplishing God's goals and directives. The Holy Spirit enables some Christians with the gift of administration to organize, direct, and implement plans to lead others in the different ministries of the Church. This gift is more directed toward goals, tasks, details, and organization.

Apostle: Taken from the Greek word *aposotolos*, it means "one sent forth," "a sent one." Such individuals are sent by God (commissioned) to be messengers/ambassadors of Jesus Christ. An apostle is also a preacher or a teacher of God's Word (2 Timothy 2:7, 2 Timothy 1:11). An apostle's ministry seems to embrace all of the other spiritual gifts; the most distinct is to establish new ministries and churches. Apostles are leaders of leaders and ministers of ministers. Such gifts can be found in church planters, some Christian scholars, and Christian institutional leaders, and people with multiple ministries or churches.

Contributor: *see* Giver.

Discerning of Spirits: This is the supernatural revelation from the Holy Spirit with the ability to distinguish between truth and error, to distinguish the influence of God and the devil in a person, statement, situation, or environment. The Greek word for the gift of discernment is *Diakrisis*.

Evangelist: One who brings the Good News; a messenger of good tidings. Their calling and message is to preach salvation through Jesus Christ to unbelievers so they respond in faith and move toward discipleship. The Bible gives wonderful examples of evangelism on an individual level (Acts 8:26-40) and in larger groups (Acts 2:14-42). All Christians are responsible to spread the Gospel. But those who have the spiritual gift of evangelism have an even greater level of responsibility because of the task God has especially equipped them to do.

Exhorter: The gift of exhortation is often called the "gift of encouragement." The Greek word for this gift is *Parakaleo*. It means to beseech, exhort, call upon, to encourage, and to strengthen. The exhorter reminds the hearer of the powerful and amazing work of God in Christ our Lord and Savior. In the Church, this gift is used to strengthen and encourage those wavering in their faith, to uplift, motivate, challenge, rebuke, and to foster spiritual growth and action.

Faith: The supernatural ability, given by the Holy Spirit, to believe God's promises, power, and presence without a doubt. The person with this gift can discern the will and power of what God wants to happen and be confident and unwavering in their belief in God's ability to fulfill His purposes, even when there is no concrete evidence.

Giver: The Holy Spirit imparts this gift to some in the Body of Christ so as to meet the needs of the Church and its ministries, missionaries, or of people who do not have the means to provide fully for themselves. Givers encourage, provide, and give all the credit to God's love and provision. The spiritual gift of giving includes monetary help, but also includes a person giving their abilities, resources, and/or time.

Healing: The supernatural ability God gives to some to serve as human instruments through which it pleases Him to cure illnesses, restore health, and destroy the works of the devil in the human body apart from the use of natural means. Some also think of the gift of healing to be applicable to not just the physical body, but also to emotional, mental, and spiritual well-being.

Helping: A person gifted in assisting others with needs.

Leader: Someone who is gifted in leadership, who is to use his or her gift with a passion to help people grow in the Lord.

Mercy: *see* Kindness

Miracles/Working of Miracles: The supernatural intervention in the ordinary course of nature which works closely with the gifts of faith and healing. The spiritual gift of miracles reveals God's power through individuals.

Pastor: Pastors are the shepherd of God's sheep in the local body of saints. Pastors are necessary for the maturing and equipping of the local body of saints. The greatest example of a shepherd is Jesus Christ.

Prophecy: Direct utterance of things to people that are not premeditated and not of human intellect but from God. Prophets and prophecy should bring forth edification (instruction, improvement), exhortation (urgent communication), or comfort (1 Corinthians 14: 3).

Prophets: *see* Prophecy

Shepherd: *see* Pastor.

Teaching: God gives this special ability to certain members of the Body of Christ to communicate a personal understanding of the Bible and faith to instruct, guide, edify, and nurture Christians in the Word of God in a way that it can be applied to life and the building up of the Church.

Various Kinds of Tongues: The supernatural ability to speak in a tongue to God and not to people (1 Corinthians 14:2). They utter mysteries by the Spirit which edify the speaker, not men. It requires another person gifted in interpreting what is said so that it can edify the Church.

Word of Knowledge: The supernatural revelation by the Holy Spirit of certain facts in the mind of God. It is the special ability that God gives to certain Christians to discover, accumulate, analyze, and clarify information and ideas that are pertinent to the growth and well-being of the body of Believers.

Word of Wisdom: The supernatural revelation by the Spirit of God concerning purpose in the mind and will of God. This gift involves having a sense of divine direction, being led by the Holy Spirit to act appropriately in a given set of circumstances, and rightly applying knowledge. The gift of wisdom is the wisdom of God. The gift of the Word of Wisdom is not natural and it cannot be gained through study or experience.

Made in the USA
Middletown, DE
17 January 2020